I Can't Believe I'm Crocheting!

We've got some really juicy insider information! It's about those hand-crocheted scarves and vests you've seen in glossy magazines. It's also about those fluffy crocheted throws that get top dollar in your favorite department store. Here's the scoop: you can crochet those great styles for yourself!

This book has all the info you need to learn the basic stitches and techniques of crochet. It doesn't matter if you're right- or left-handed, because the how-to-stitch photos are shown both ways. Just watch for the **Hands On** alerts that will keep you pointed in the right direction, and check out the **FAQs** when you find you have a question. You'll soon be able to make retro dishcloths, a baby blanket, decorator afghans, or a cute koala. And of course, you get instructions to make two vests, a scarf, and a felted purse. Now that you can crochet accessories like those budget-busting fashions you've been craving, don't be surprised when your friends want to know where you've been shopping!

48

49

50

52

61

58

55

CROCHET BASICS

The Crochet Basics section photo figs are provided for both right-handed and left-handed crocheters. If you are left-handed, please be sure to read the special note to lefties on page 29 once you have become familiar with the basic stitches.

hands on

You'll need a hook, size H (5 mm) and a ball or skein of medium weight yarn. Look for an icon on the yarn label like this (MEDIUM 4). When choosing the yarn, you may be drawn to all the fabulous fuzzy or variegated yarns, but save those for later. You'll find that working with a light or bright color and a smooth yarn will make your stitches easier to see. You'll also need scissors and a tape measure. Before starting, take a look at the photo of the crochet hook on page 31. Some of the terms on the photo— throat, working area— will be used in the following instructions.

So, grab your hook and yarn and let's start crocheting!

FAQ

Grab a hook? How?

ANSWER

Hold it like a pencil or a mixing spoon. Look at the photos below. You may find that one way is easier with smaller hooks and the other with larger hooks. Try out both methods and choose the one that feels best for you.

Method 1: You may hold the hook in the same position as you would a pencil with the hook resting on top of your hand ***(Fig. 1a)***.

Fig. 1a Right-handed

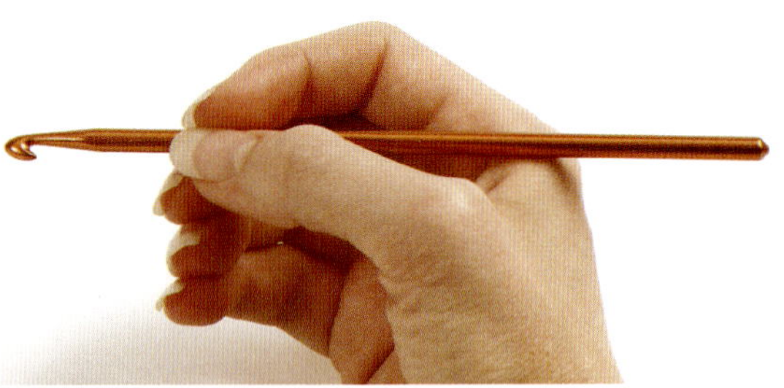

Left-handed

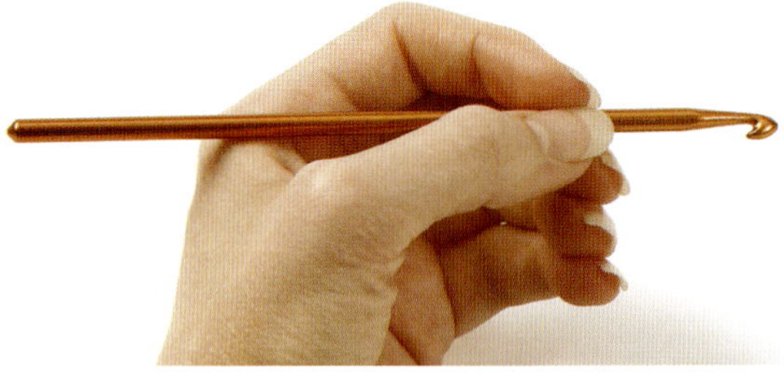

Method 2: You may grasp the hook with your fingers around it ***(Fig. 1b)***, similar to holding a mixing spoon.

Fig. 1b Right-handed

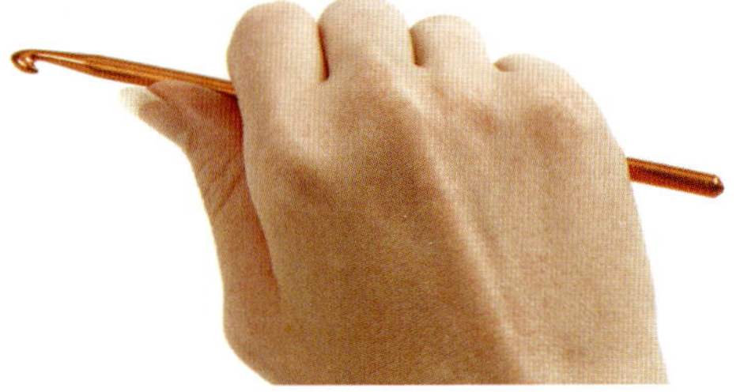

Left-handed

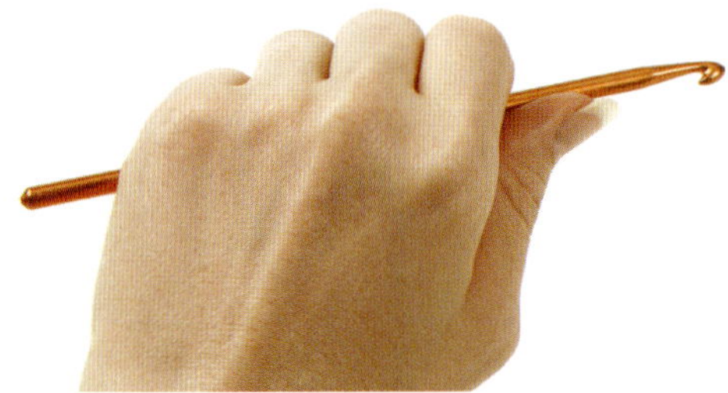

MAKING A SLIP KNOT

The first thing that goes on your hook will be a slip knot. The grown-up and current Scouts reading this probably remember how to make one of these adjustable knots. If not, here's a simple way to do it.

Pull a 6" (15 cm) length of yarn from the ball. Make a circle at the 6" (15 cm) spot and put the circle on top of the yarn that comes from the ball ***(Fig. 2a)***. The yarn that comes from the ball is the ***working yarn***.

Fig. 2a Right-handed

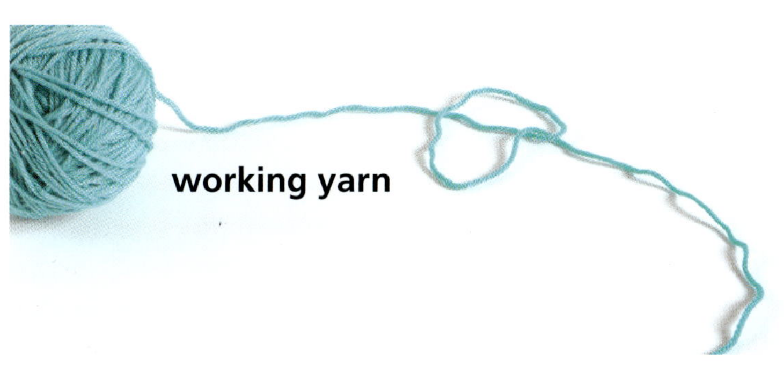

Left-handed

Slip the hook under the working yarn ***(Fig. 2b)*** and pull on both strands of the yarn to tighten the slip knot ***(Fig. 2c)***. The loop should slide easily up and down the working area of your hook. Don't worry if you pull too tightly—remember, it's adjustable. Just pull upward on the loop to make it larger.

Fig. 2b Right-handed

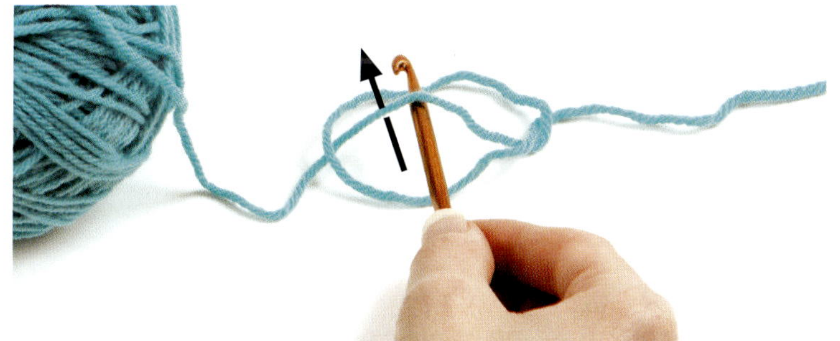

Left-handed

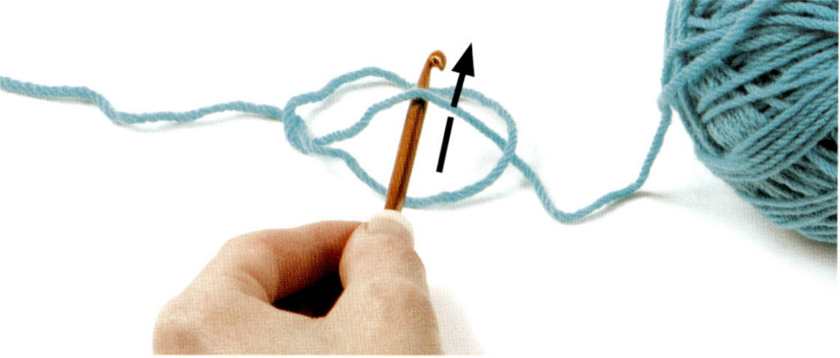

Fig. 2c Right-handed

Left-handed

HOLDING THE YARN

You have the hook, you have the slip knot, now what? Your other hand, the one not holding the hook, has something to learn—how to hold the yarn.

FAQ

Can't I just let the yarn hang there?
I don't know if I can get that hand to cooperate!

ANSWER

Look at the hands below. The area between the loop on the hook and your index finger will be the yarn that you will crochet. If it is allowed to just hang, the stitches you form will be uneven and pretty sloppy. Your other hand has an important job, controlling the size of your stitches. You may find a way to hold the yarn and hook that's different from what's shown here, and that's okay. The idea is to control them in a way that allows the yarn to slide smoothly and evenly through your hand to the hook.

With the hook in your preferred hand, hold the slip knot with the thumb and middle finger of your other hand. Loop the working yarn over the index finger of that hand and grasp it in the palm with your ring and little fingers ***(Fig. 3)***.

Fig. 3 Right-handed

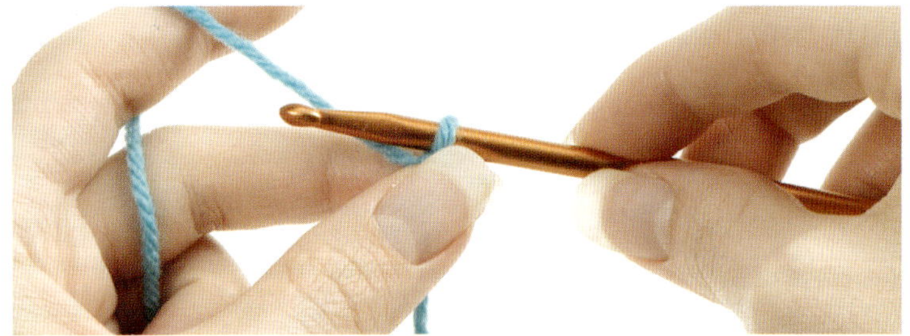

Left-handed

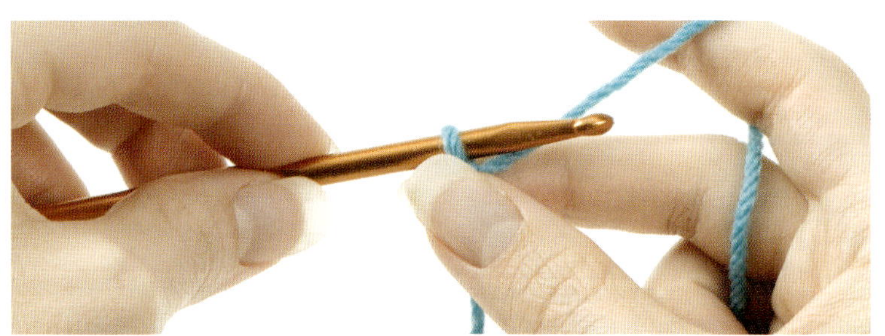

YO, LET'S GET GOING

To start out crocheting, you need to make a chain stitch. But **before** the chain, you need to learn how to yarn over ***(abbreviated YO)***. Every crochet stitch uses at least one yarn over in the steps of making the stitch.

Bring the yarn **over** the hook from the **back** to the **front**. Turn the hook to catch the yarn with the throat area ***(see Anatomy of a Hook, page 31)***, so the yarn won't slip off ***(Fig. 4)***.

Fig. 4 Right-handed

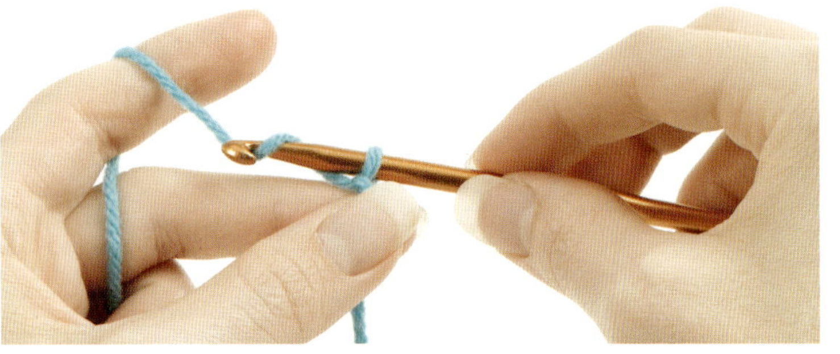

Left-handed

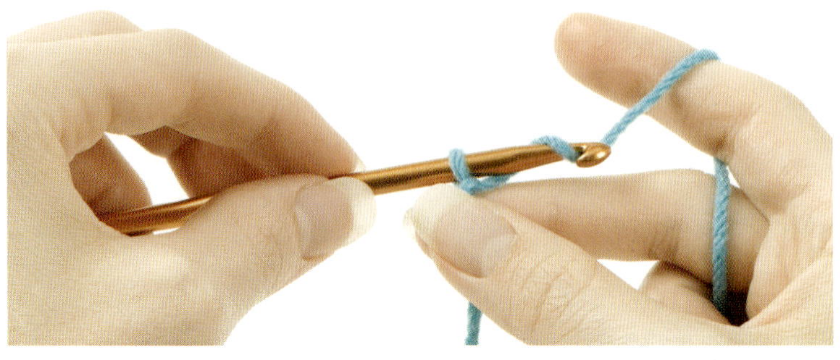

HOW TO MAKE A CHAIN (abbreviated ch)

Let's do something with the yarn over you have on your hook. The yarn over is the first step to all crochet stitches, including this one—the chain.

Draw the hook with the yarn around the throat thru the loop that is on the working area ***(Fig. 5a)***. That's one chain and you will still have a loop on the hook ***(Fig. 5b)***. Don't leave the loop on the throat area; slide it on back to the working area to open up the loop. You'll need to be able to put your hook back thru the chain later on, so work your chains even and loose enough to do that.

Fig. 5a Right-handed **Left-handed**

Fig. 5b Right-handed **Left-handed**

To form your stitches correctly, bring the yarn over the hook from **back** to **front** as shown in **Fig. 6a**, not from front to back as shown in **Fig. 6b**.

Fig. 6a Right-handed **Left-handed**

Fig. 6b Right-handed **Left-handed**

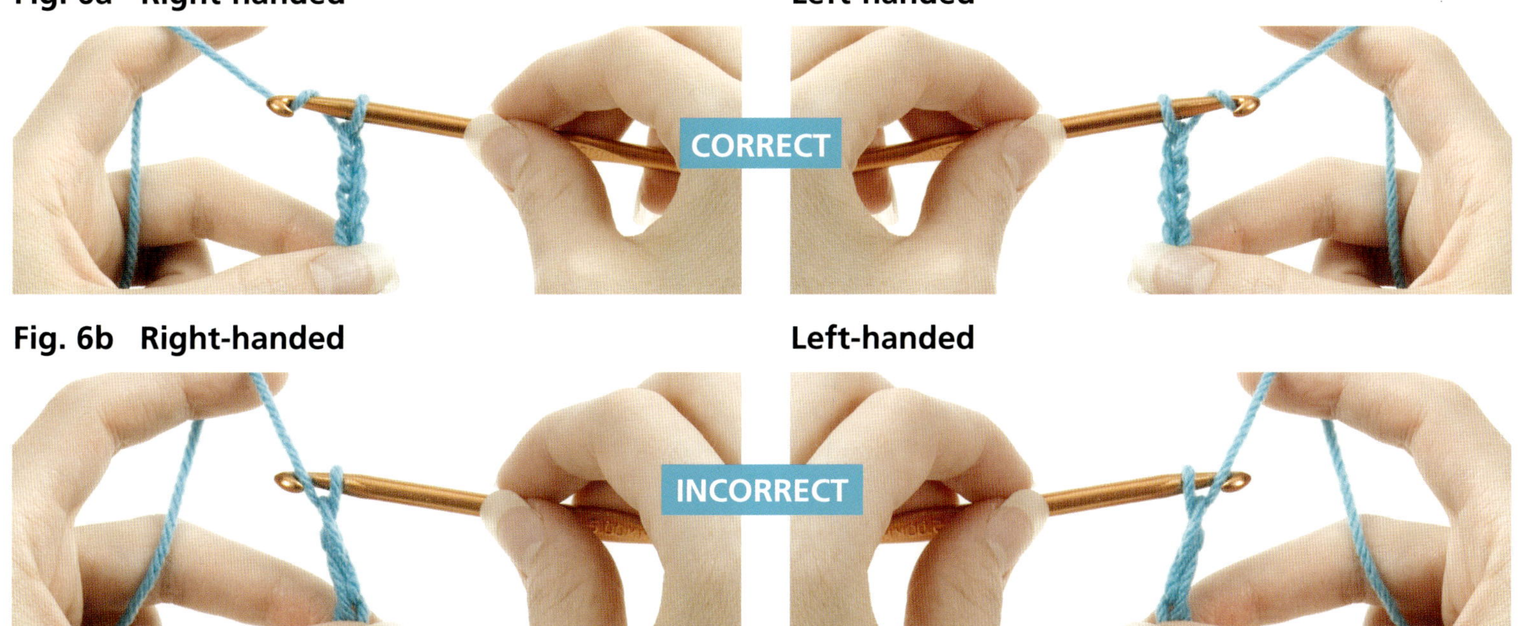

FAQ

EEK! My hook fell out!

ANSWER

Don't panic. If the hook slips out of your work, just slip it back through the front of the stitch without twisting the loop ***(Fig. 7)***.

Fig. 7 Right-handed

Left-handed

Since you are new to crochet, you may have a tendency to work too tightly. Just take it easy and work loosely. (After all, this is supposed to be relaxing!) It's better at first to have your work a little too loose than too tight. The more you practice, the better your control of the yarn will become which, in turn, will make your stitches more even.

MORE CHAINS

To make each additional chain, bring the yarn over the hook and draw through the loop on hook. To count your chains, begin with the first chain after the hook and then count back towards the beginning of your foundation chain, the slip knot ***(Fig. 8)***.

Fig. 8 Right-handed

Left-handed

As your chain grows longer, let it slip through your fingers, moving your thumb and finger up and keeping them close to the hook ***(Fig. 9a)***. If you work holding too far down the chain ***(Fig. 9b)***, your newest chains will not have the same tension or be the same size as the first ones.

Fig. 9a   Right-handed **Left-handed**

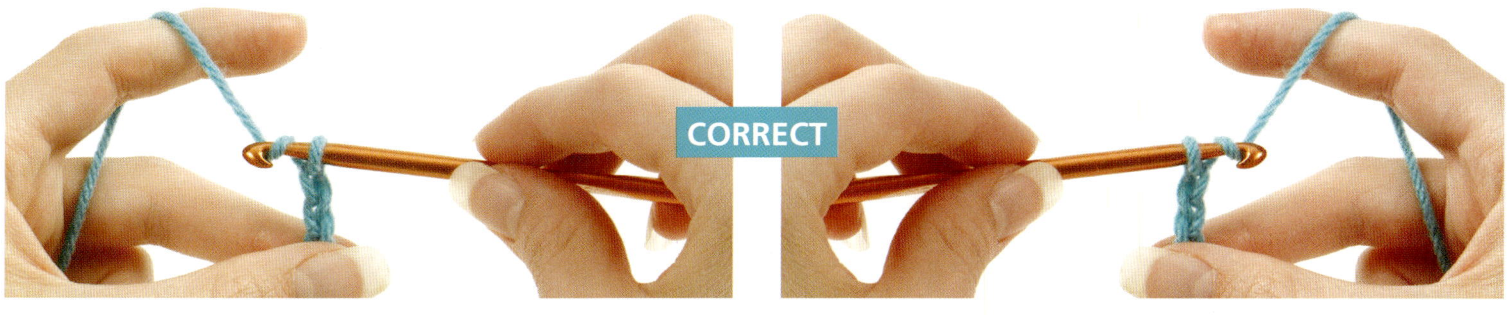

Fig. 9b   Right-handed **Left-handed**

hands on

Work until you feel comfortable making a chain and your stitches are neat and even. Since you are practicing just making a chain, when you are finished; cut the yarn, slip the hook out of the last loop, and pull the end through to secure it.

Turn the page for some more info about chains.

CHAINING LOOSELY

Your beginning chain for a project should be worked loosely to allow you to work the first row easily into those foundation chains. Here are a few ways to tell if your chains are loose enough:

1. The loop formed on your hook for each chain stays the same size as the working area of the hook.
2. The loop has not shrunk down to the size of the hook's throat ***(Fig. 45, page 31)***.
3. If you have to use force to push the hook back through a chain, then you have made your chains too tight. In that case, just rip it back and try to work your chains a little looser.

It is **very important** that the loop remains the same size as the working area of the hook you are using.

WORKING INTO THE CHAIN

Compare the chain you made to the one in **Figs. 10a & b**. The front of the chain looks like a series of "V's" and the back side has bumps that are called the back ridge.

Fig. 10a **Right-handed** **FRONT** **Left-handed** **FRONT**

Fig. 10b **Right-handed** **BACK** **Left-handed** **BACK**

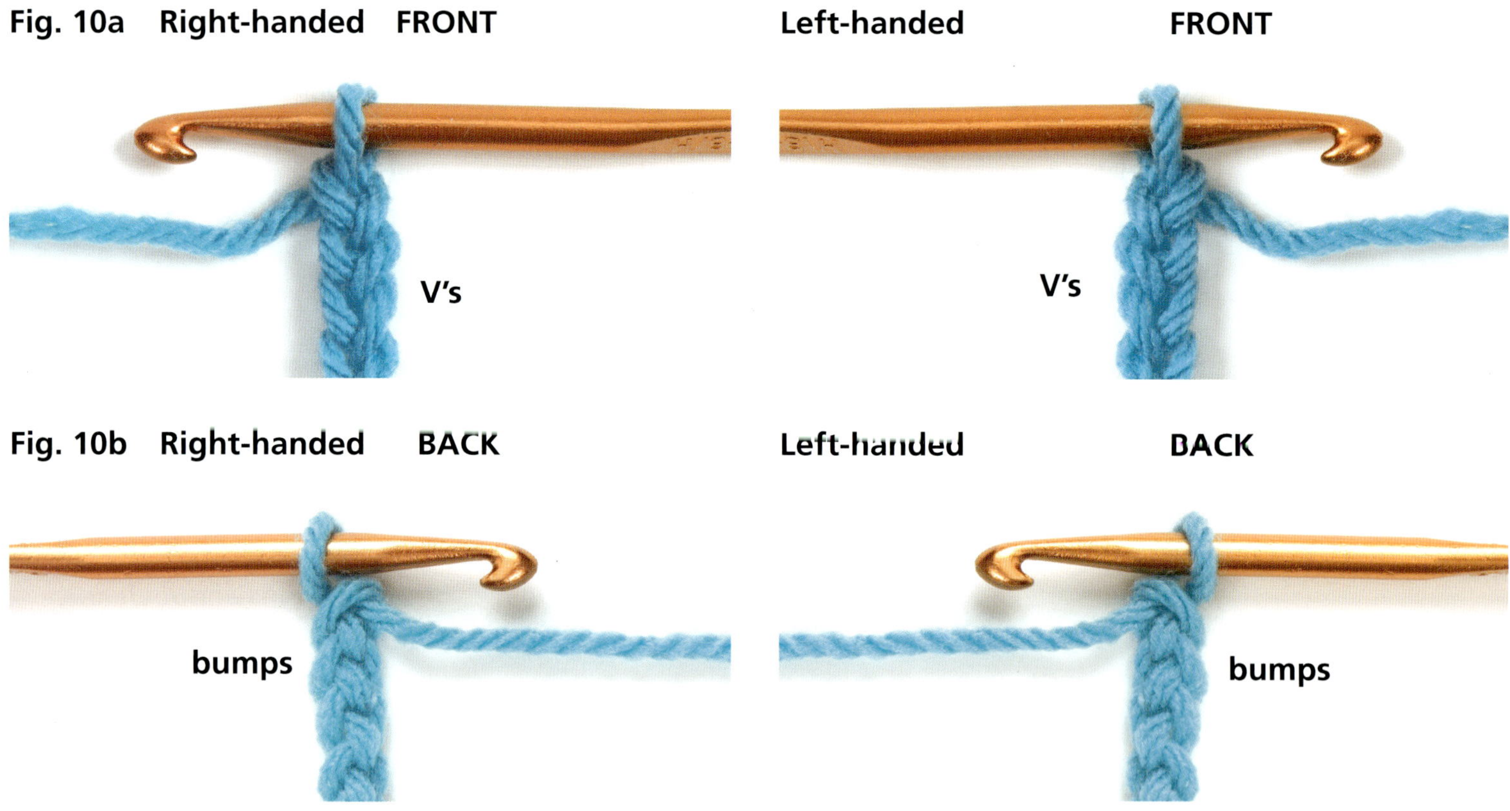

When your beginning chain is complete, crochet stitches will then be worked into the individual chains. There are two different methods for doing this.

Method 1: WORKING INTO THE BACK RIDGE OF A CHAIN
Insert the hook into the back ridge only of each chain ***(Fig. 11a)***.

Fig. 11a Right-handed **Left-handed**

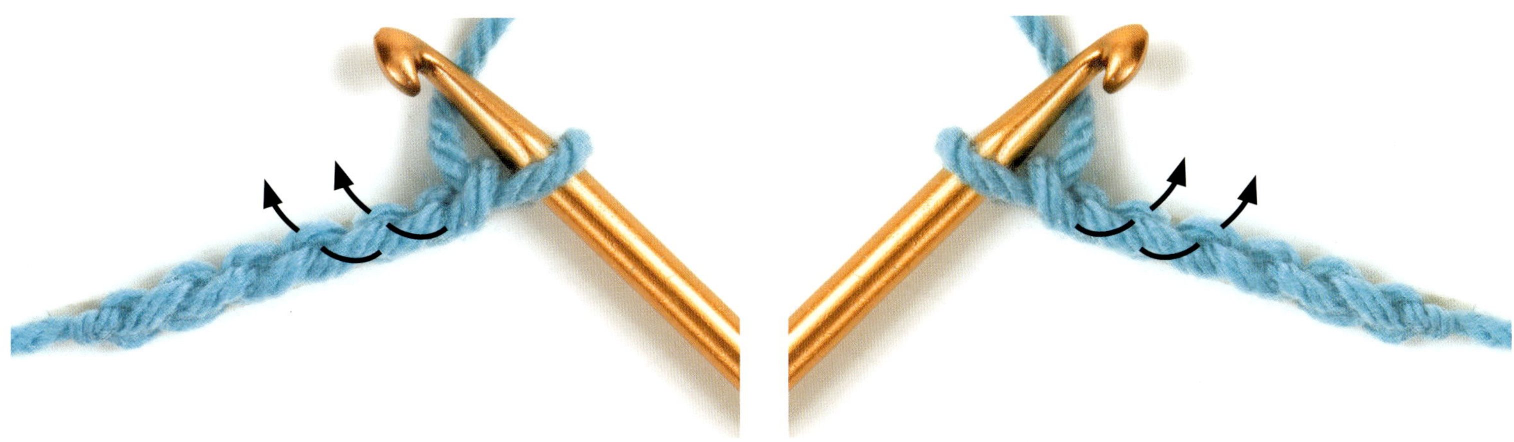

Method 2: WORKING INTO THE TOP TWO LOOPS OF A CHAIN
Insert the hook under the top strand **and** the back ridge of each chain ***(Fig. 11b)***.

Fig. 11b Right-handed **Left-handed**

Working into the back ridge of a chain gives the piece a smoother edge. Some patterns will specify using the back ridge. For those that do not, feel free to use either method. Whichever method you choose, use that one all the way through the same project so the edges will look the same.

BASIC STITCHES

Learning the basic stitches (or any other crochet stitch) is just an extension of how you made a chain. You will hold the yarn and the hook as you have before and will bring the yarn over the hook in the same way. In addition to the chain, most crochet designs use a combination of one or more of these five basic stitches: **slip stitch**, **single crochet**, **half double crochet**, **double crochet**, and **treble crochet**. Each stitch is made with one or more yarn overs and is completed by drawing the hook through the loop or loops on the hook. How many loops you have on the hook to draw through is what varies the height of the stitches ***(Fig. 12)***.

Fig. 12 Right-handed **Left-handed**

Treble crochet
Double crochet
Half double crochet
Single crochet
Slip stitch

SINGLE CROCHET *(abbreviated sc)*

To practice making single crochets, let's work a sample swatch, starting with a beginning chain.

Chain 17 stitches **loosely**.

ROW 1

Step 1: Insert the hook in the **second** chain from the hook, using one of the methods for working into a chain ***(Figs. 11a or b, page 9)***.

Step 2: Bring the yarn over the hook and pull up a loop through the chain ***(Fig. 13a)***. Stop there, don't pull it through the loop on the hook. You now have 2 loops on the hook.

Fig. 13a Right-handed **Left-handed**

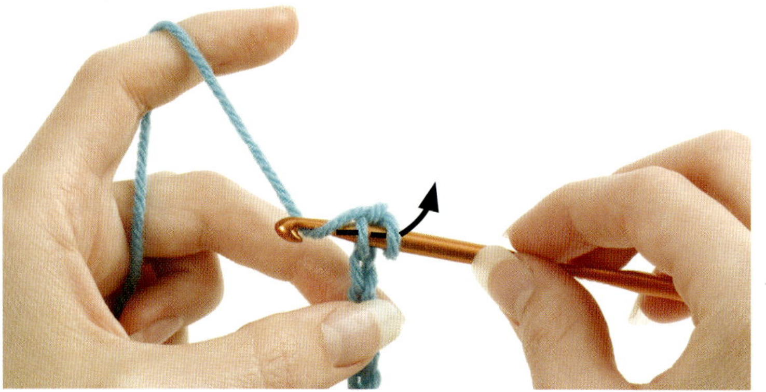

Step 3: Bring the yarn over the hook and draw the hook through **both** of the loops ***(Fig. 13b)***.

Fig. 13b Right-handed

Left-handed

CONGRATULATIONS!
You have made a single crochet ***(Fig. 13c)***, and one loop will remain on the hook.

Fig. 13c Right-handed

Left-handed

Note: As you crochet, you will always have one loop remaining on your hook after completing a stitch.

Step 4: Insert the hook in the next chain, using the same method as before.

Step 5: Bring the yarn over the hook and pull up a loop through the chain (2 loops on hook).

Step 6: Bring the yarn over the hook and draw the hook through both loops **(single crochet made)**.

Repeat Steps 4-6 in each chain across, making sure not to twist the beginning chain as you work.

You should now have one row of 16 single crochets.

Stop a moment and take a look at the top of the single crochets. Each single crochet has two horizontal strands or loops that form the top of the stitch and look like a horizontal "V," very similar to a chain. These are the loops you will put your hook under to work the next row.

To begin the next row of single crochets, you need to make a **turning chain** to raise the yarn to the height of a single crochet, and then turn your work around so you can crochet back across the first row. The turning chain for a single crochet is one chain. This chain is used **only** to gain height; it is not counted as the first single crochet.

Single crochet continued on page 12.

ROW 2
Step 1: Chain one stitch ***(Fig. 14,* turning chain made)**.

Fig. 14 Right-handed

Left-handed

Step 2: Turn your work around ***(Fig. 15)***. Right-handed crocheters will rotate the work to their left and the left-handed will rotate the work to their right.

Fig. 15 Right-handed

Left-handed

Step 3: Insert the hook **under both** top loops of the first single crochet (the single crochet closest to the hook) ***(Fig. 16)***.

Fig. 16 Right-handed

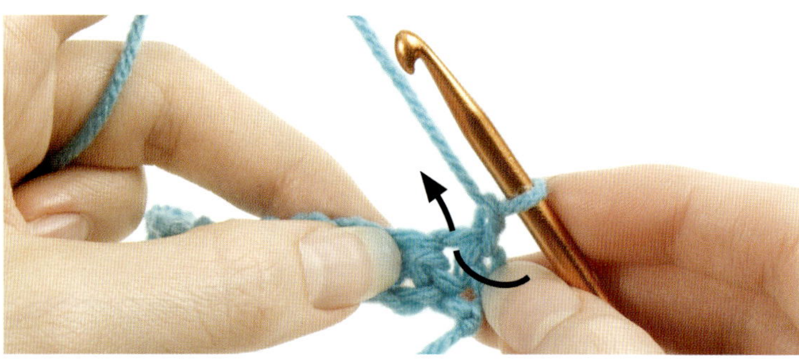

Left-handed

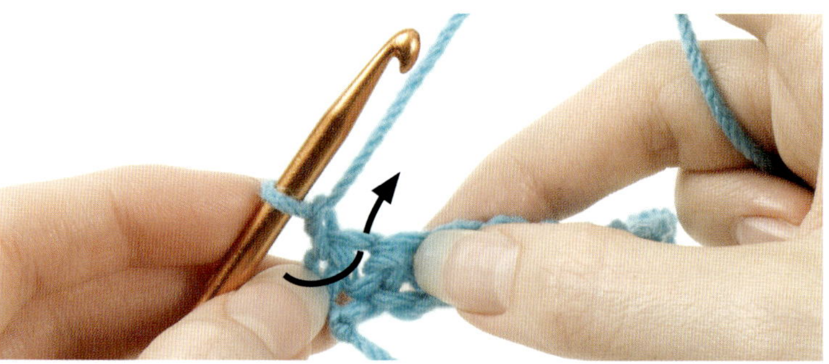

Step 4: Bring the yarn over the hook and pull up a loop (2 loops on hook).

Step 5: Bring the yarn over the hook and draw the hook through both loops **(single crochet made)**.

Step 6: Work a single crochet in each of the remaining single crochets across the row. You should still have 16 single crochets. If you don't, check the last stitch.

Make sure you worked into the last single crochet of the row because it is very easy to miss it ***(Fig. 17)***.

Fig. 17 Right-handed

Left-handed

ROW 3

Repeat Steps 1-6 of Row 2. Remember, don't work into the turning chain since it doesn't count as a stitch ***(Fig. 18)***.

Fig. 18 Right-handed

Left-handed

hands on

Continue practicing rows of single crochets until you are comfortable with these steps. **Fig. 19** shows a swatch of single crochets.

Fig. 19 Right-handed

Left-handed

Don't put down that swatch—
let's learn the slip stitch!

SLIP STITCH (abbreviated slip st)

This stitch is used to move the yarn across a group of stitches, to attach new yarn, or to join work. Slip stitches don't add much height to your work.

Let's use your swatch to practice making slip stitches.

Step 1: Turn your work, then insert the hook **under both** top loops of the first single crochet ***(Figs. 15 & 16, page 12)***. Bring the yarn over the hook and draw the hook through the stitch **and** the loop on the hook ***(Fig. 20a)***.

Fig. 20a Right-handed **Left-handed**

CONGRATULATIONS!
You have made a slip stitch ***(Fig. 20b)***, and one loop will remain on the hook.

Fig. 20b Right-handed **Left-handed**

Step 2: Insert the hook in the next single crochet, bring the yarn over the hook and draw the hook through the stitch **and** the loop on the hook **(slip stitch made)**.

Repeat Step 2 in each single crochet across; then follow the next section to learn how to finish off.

FINISH OFF

When you complete your last stitch, cut the yarn leaving a 4-6" (10-15 cm) end. Bring the loose end through the last loop on your hook and tighten it ***(Fig. 21)***.

Fig. 21 Right-handed

Left-handed

This secures the end so the stitches won't unravel. This technique is referred to as **finish off**, **fasten off**, or **end off** in most instructions.

If you find that your yarn is too slippery or stiff to stay secure with this ending, then make an extra chain after your last stitch and pull the loose end through that chain.

HALF DOUBLE CROCHET (abbreviated hdc)

The half double crochet is the next step up and is slightly taller than a single crochet.

To practice making half double crochets, let's work another sample swatch. Start with a beginning chain.

Chain 17 stitches **loosely**.

ROW 1

Step 1: Bring the yarn over the hook, skip the first two chains, and insert the hook in the **third** chain from the hook ***(Fig. 22a)***, keeping the new loop (the yarn over) on the hook.

Fig. 22a Right-handed

Left-handed

Half double crochet continued on page 16.

Step 2: Bring the yarn over the hook and pull up a loop through the chain ***(Fig. 22b)***. Stop there, don't draw the hook through the loops on the hook yet. You now have 3 loops on the hook.

Fig. 22b Right-handed

Left-handed

Step 3: Bring the yarn over the hook and draw the hook through **all** 3 loops on the hook at once ***(Fig. 22c)***.

Fig. 22c Right-handed

Left-handed

CONGRATULATIONS!
You have made a half double crochet ***(Fig. 22d)***, and one loop will remain on the hook.

Fig. 22d Right-handed

Left-handed

Step 4: Bring the yarn over the hook and insert hook in the next chain.

Step 5: Bring the yarn over the hook and pull up a loop (3 loops on hook).

Step 6: Bring the yarn over the hook and draw the hook through all 3 loops **(half double crochet made)**.

Repeat Steps 4-6 across the chain.

You should have 15 half double crochets plus the two chains skipped at the beginning of the row (which count as one stitch) for a total of 16 stitches. The first two chains are skipped to gain row height so the first half double crochet can stand up straight.

To begin the next row of half double crochets, you must first make a **turning chain** to raise the yarn to the height of a half double crochet, and then turn the work around so you can crochet back across the first row.

The turning chain for a half double crochet is two chains, the same as the number of skipped chains on the first row. These chains serve two purposes; they gain row height **and** count as the first half double crochet of the row.

ROW 2

Step 1: Chain 2 stitches, then turn your work around ***(Fig. 23,* turning chain made) (counts as first half double crochet)**.

Fig. 23 Right-handed

Left-handed

Step 2: Bring the yarn over the hook, skip the first half double crochet and insert the hook **under both** top loops of the next half double crochet ***(Fig. 24)***.

Fig. 24 Right-handed

Left-handed

Step 3: Bring the yarn over the hook and pull up a loop (3 loops on hook).

Step 4: Bring the yarn over the hook and draw the hook through all 3 loops **(half double crochet made)**.

Half double crochet continued on page 18.

Step 5: Work a half double crochet in each of the remaining half double crochets across the row, working the last half double crochet in top of the beginning chain ***(Fig. 25)***.

Fig. 25 Right-handed

Left-handed

Counting the turning chain, you now have 16 half double crochets.

ROW 3

Repeat Steps 1-5 of Row 2, working the last half double crochet into the top of the turning chain ***(Fig. 26)***.

Fig. 26 Right-handed

Left-handed

hands on

Continue practicing rows of half double crochets until you are comfortable with these steps, then finish off your work. **Fig. 27** shows a swatch of half double crochets.

Fig. 27 Right-handed

Left-handed

DOUBLE CROCHET (abbreviated dc)

This stitch is made in the same manner as a half double crochet but with an extra step. A double crochet is slightly taller than a half double crochet and twice as tall as a single crochet.

Let's work another swatch to learn how to make double crochets. Start with a beginning chain.

Chain 18 stitches **loosely**.

ROW 1

Step 1: Bring the yarn over the hook, skip the first three chains, and insert the hook in the **fourth** chain from the hook ***(Fig. 28a)***, keeping the new loop (the yarn over) on the hook.

Fig. 28a Right-handed

Left-handed

Step 2: Bring the yarn over the hook and pull up a loop through the chain ***(Fig. 28b)***. Stop there, don't pull it through the loops on the hook. You now have 3 loops on the hook.

Fig. 28b Right-handed

Left-handed

Step 3: Bring the yarn over the hook and draw the hook through the **first** 2 loops on the hook. You now have 2 loops remaining on the hook ***(Fig. 28c)***.

Fig. 28c Right-handed

Left-handed

Double crochet continued on page 20.

Step 4: Bring the yarn over the hook and draw the hook through the **remaining** 2 loops ***(Fig. 28d)***.

Fig. 28d Right-handed

Left-handed

CONGRATULATIONS!
You have made a double crochet ***(Fig. 28e)***, and one loop will remain on the hook.

Fig. 28e Right-handed

Left-handed

Step 5: Bring the yarn over the hook and insert the hook in the next chain.

Step 6: Bring the yarn over the hook and pull up a loop (3 loops on hook).

Step 7: Bring the yarn over the hook and draw the hook through the first 2 loops (2 loops remain on hook).

Step 8: Bring the yarn over the hook and draw the hook through the remaining 2 loops **(double crochet made)**.

Repeat Steps 5-8 across the chain.

You should have 15 double crochets plus the three chains at the beginning of the row (which count as the first stitch) for a total of 16 stitches. The first three chains are skipped to gain row height so the first double crochet can stand up straight.

To begin the next row of double crochets, you make a **turning chain** first to raise the yarn to the height of a double crochet, and then turn the work around so you can crochet back across the first row. The turning chain for a double crochet is three chains, the same as the skipped chains on the first row. These chains provide row height **and** also count as the first double crochet of the row.

ROW 2

Step 1: Chain 3 stitches, then turn your work around ***(Fig. 29,* turning chain made) (counts as first double crochet)**.

Fig. 29 Right-handed

Left-handed

Step 2: Bring the yarn over the hook, skip the first double crochet and insert the hook **under both** top loops of the next double crochet ***(Fig. 30)***.

Fig. 30 Right-handed

Left-handed

Step 3: Bring the yarn over the hook and pull up a loop (3 loops on hook).

Step 4: Bring the yarn over the hook and draw the hook through the first 2 loops (2 loops remain on hook).

Step 5: Bring the yarn over the hook and draw the hook through the remaining 2 loops **(double crochet made)**.

Step 6: Work a double crochet in each of the remaining double crochets across the row, working the last double crochet in top of the beginning chain ***(Fig. 31)***.

Fig. 31 Right-handed

Left-handed

Counting the turning chain, you now have 16 double crochets.

Double crochet continued on page 22.

ROW 3
Repeat Steps 1-6 of Row 2, working the last double crochet into the turning chain ***(Fig. 26, page 18)***.

hands on

Continue practicing rows of double crochets until you are comfortable with these steps, then finish off your work. **Fig. 32** shows a swatch of double crochets.

Fig. 32 Right-handed

Left-handed

TREBLE CROCHET *(abbreviated tr)*

The treble crochet is taller than all the previous stitches you have learned so far. Like the double crochet, it is worked by drawing through 2 loops on your hook until all the loops are gone (except for the one that always remains on your hook).

Start with a beginning chain for a swatch to learn how to make treble crochets.

Chain 19 stitches **loosely**.

ROW 1
Step 1: Bring the yarn over the hook **twice**, skip the first four chains, and insert the hook in the **fifth** chain from the hook ***(Fig. 33a)***, keeping both new loops (the yarn overs) on the hook.

Fig. 33a Right-handed

Left-handed

Step 2: Bring the yarn over the hook and pull up a loop through the chain ***(Fig. 33b)***. Stop there, don't pull it through the loops on the hook. You now have 4 loops on the hook.

Fig. 33b Right-handed

Left-handed

Step 3: Bring the yarn over the hook and draw the hook through the **first** 2 loops. You now have 3 loops remaining on the hook ***(Fig. 33c)***.

Fig. 33c Right-handed

Left-handed

Step 4: Bring the yarn over the hook and draw the hook through the **next** 2 loops ***(Fig. 33d)***. You now have 2 loops remaining on the hook.

Fig. 33d Right-handed

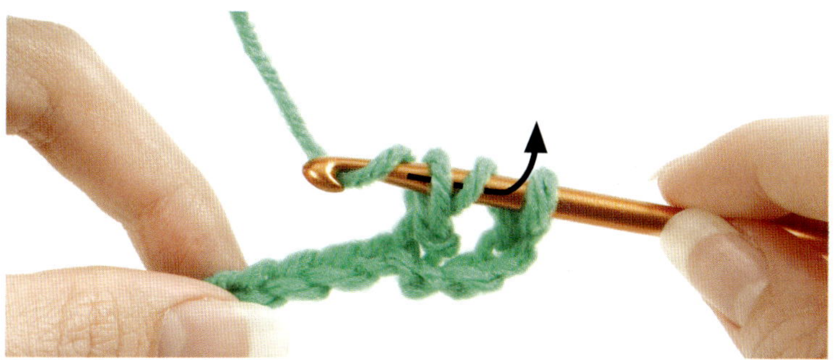

Left-handed

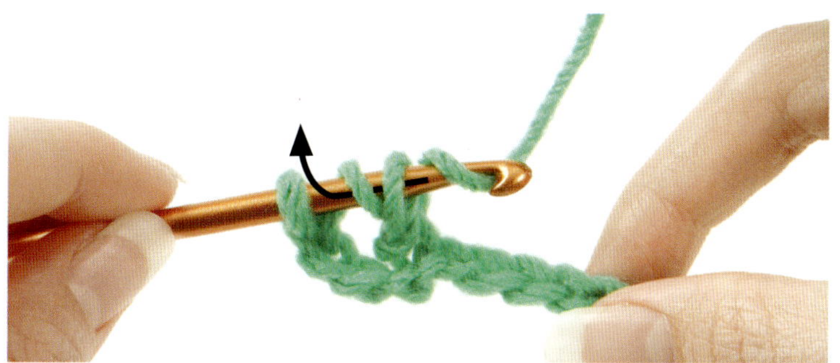

Treble crochet continued on page 24.

Step 5: Bring the yarn over the hook and draw the hook through the **remaining** 2 loops ***(Fig. 33e)***.

Fig. 33e Right-handed

Left-handed

CONGRATULATIONS!
You have made a treble crochet ***(Fig. 33f)***, and one loop will remain on the hook.

Fig. 33f Right-handed

Left-handed

Step 6: Bring the yarn over the hook twice and insert hook in the next chain.

Step 7: Bring the yarn over the hook and pull up a loop (4 loops on hook).

Step 8: Bring the yarn over the hook and draw through the first 2 loops (3 loops remain on hook).

Step 9: Bring the yarn over the hook and draw through the next 2 loops (2 loops remain on hook).

Step 10: Bring the yarn over the hook and draw through the remaining 2 loops **(treble crochet made)**.

Repeat Steps 6-10 across the chain.

You should have 15 treble crochets plus the four chains at the beginning of the row (which count as one stitch) for a total of 16 stitches. The first four chains are skipped to gain row height so the first treble crochet can stand up straight.

To begin the next row of treble crochets, you must first make a **turning chain** to raise the yarn to the height of a treble crochet, and then turn the work around so you can crochet back across the first row.

The turning chain for a treble crochet is four chains, the same as the skipped chains on the first row. These chains provide both row height **and** count as the first treble crochet of the row.

ROW 2

Step 1: Chain 4 stitches, then turn your work around ***(Fig. 34,* turning chain made) (counts as first treble crochet)**.

Fig. 34 Right-handed

Left-handed

Step 2: Bring the yarn over the hook twice, skip the first treble crochet and insert the hook **under both** top loops of the next treble crochet ***(Fig. 35)***.

Fig. 35 Right-handed

Left-handed

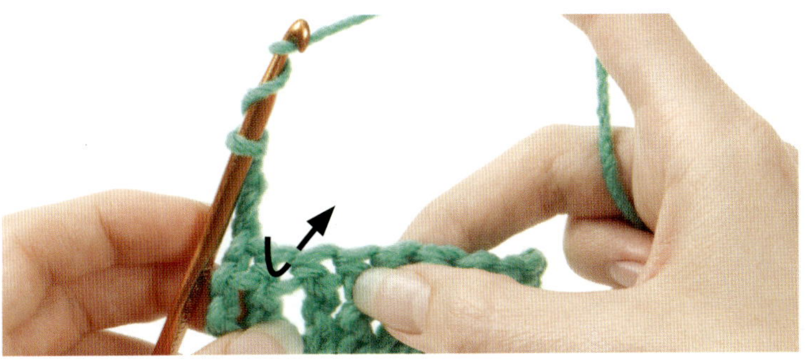

Step 3: Bring the yarn over the hook and pull up a loop (4 loops on hook).

Step 4: Bring the yarn over the hook and draw the hook through the first 2 loops (3 loops remain on hook).

Step 5: Bring the yarn over the hook and draw the hook through the next 2 loops (2 loops remain on hook).

Step 6: Bring the yarn over the hook and draw the hook through the remaining 2 loops **(treble crochet made)**.

Treble crochet continued on page 26.

Step 7: Work a treble crochet in each of the remaining treble crochets across the row, working the last treble crochet in top of the beginning chain ***(Fig. 36)***.

Fig. 36 Right-handed

Left-handed

Counting the turning chain, you now have 16 treble crochets.

ROW 3

Repeat Steps 1-7 of Row 2, working the last treble crochet into the turning chain ***(Fig. 26, page 18)***.

hands on

Continue practicing rows of treble crochets until you are comfortable with these steps, then finish off your work. **Fig. 37** shows a swatch of treble crochets.

Fig. 37 Right-handed

Left-handed

TURNING CHAINS

You may have noticed that most of the basic stitches need a turning chain at the beginning of each row or round to gain the height necessary for making your next stitch. The one exception is the slip stitch which doesn't have much height. The turning chain should be equal in height to the stitch you are going to use in a particular row or round ***(Fig. 38)***.

Fig. 38 Right-handed **Left-handed**

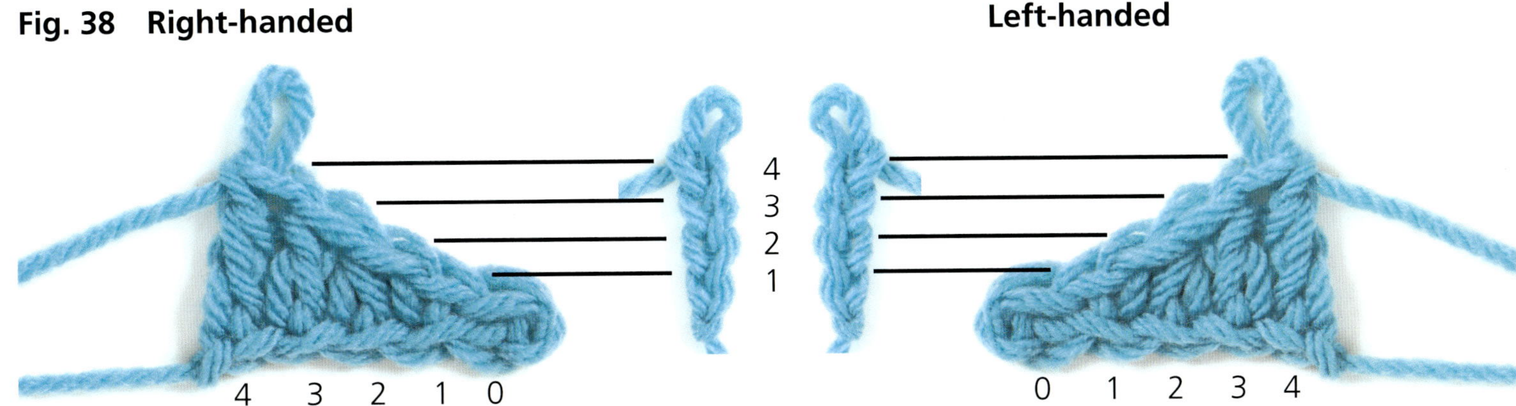

0 - Slip stitch
1 - Single crochet
2 - Half double crochet
3 - Double crochet
4 - Treble crochet

A single crochet is the same height as one chain. This is the turning chain that gains row or round height **only**; it does **not** count as the first single crochet.

A half double crochet is the same height as two chains, a double crochet is the same height as three chains, and a treble crochet is the same height as four chains. For these taller stitches, the turning chain usually counts as the first stitch of that row or round.

FAQ

Rounds have been mentioned a couple of times, so tell me, how *do* I work something round?

ANSWER

So far, all the crochet you have been doing has been in rows; working across, then turning your work for another row. Working in rows will produce rectangular or square pieces. When crochet is worked in a circular fashion instead of back and forth in rows, it will produce a round piece, unless you increase to create corners. To start a round, you either begin with a loop or ring and then work the stitches into the loop or the ring. Check out the next two pages for examples of working crochet in the round.

WORKING IN THE ROUND

MAKING A BEGINNING LOOP

A beginning loop starts with a beginning chain, and all the stitches for the first round are worked into the last chain from the hook (just above the slip knot). **Fig. 39** shows one example, a chain-4 with double crochets worked in the fourth chain from the hook.

Fig. 39 Right-handed

Left-handed

MAKING A BEGINNING RING

A beginning ring is used when you need more stitches on the first round than a beginning loop will hold. To form a beginning ring, work the specified number of chains and then join to the first chain made with a slip stitch ***(Fig. 40)***. This method will leave an open center and stitches may be worked either in the actual ring or in the chains of the ring. If stitches will be worked in the chains, be careful not to get the chain twisted when joining.

Fig. 40 Right-handed

Left-handed

CONTINUOUS ROUNDS

Continuous rounds are primarily used in single crochet and are worked without joining or turning (in a continuous spiral fashion) ***(Fig. 41)***. To keep track of rounds, a marker is placed at the beginning of each round and is moved after each round is complete ***(see Markers, page 40)***.

Fig. 41 Right-handed

Left-handed

ROUNDS WITHOUT TURNING

In this technique, at the end of each round, the yarn is joined with a slip stitch ***(Figs. 20a & b, page 14)*** to the top of the beginning chain or to the first stitch, but the piece is **not** turned at the beginning of the next round. With this method there is a definite visible joining line which moves slightly toward the right or left in a spiral ***(Fig. 42)***. This cannot be avoided and is the reason garments are often designed in two pieces with side seams or worked in rounds with turning (below). ***Note:*** The photos have been color enhanced to show the first stitch.

Fig. 42 Right-handed

Left-handed

ROUNDS WITH TURNING

For rounds with turning, at the end of each round, the yarn is joined with a slip stitch ***(Figs. 20a & b, page 14)*** to the top of the beginning chain or to the first stitch, and then the piece is turned at the beginning of the next round. The visible joining line will remain straight in this method ***(Fig. 43)***.

Fig. 43 Right-handed

Left-handed

NOTE TO THE LEFTIES

Have you noticed that the only difference between the left-handed stitches and the right-handed stitches is the direction that they are worked and the slant that they tend to lean? Go ahead, take another look. Otherwise, the stitches are the same, just mirror images of each other. And, speaking of mirrors, when you encounter a right-handed fig. or photo in the rest of this book, just prop a mirror next to it to see the stitches left-handed. The one other thing you must consider is garment shaping. Since most instructions are written right-handed (sorry), the Right Front instructions will turn out to be your Left Front and vice versa. Since you crochet from left to right, you may need to reverse some instructions.

Turn the page for a look at some neat necessities!

CROCHET NECESSITIES

Note: A list of materials needed for beginners is located on page 2 in the ***hands on*** paragraph.

Crochet requires only a few essentials, and the next few pages will show what you need to get started. Different types of hooks and yarns will be explained, and a variety of crocheting accessories will be covered.

Fig. 44

HOOKS

Let's first take a look at the structure of a crochet hook, and then go on to see the different materials that they can be made from.

ANATOMY OF A CROCHET HOOK

A crochet hook can be divided into five different sections, with each section having its own purpose ***(Fig. 45)***.

Fig. 45

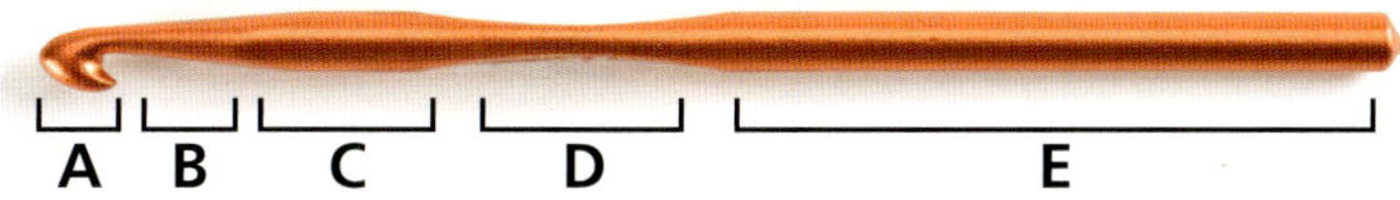

A. Hook - end used to catch yarn and pull it through other loops.
B. Throat - shaped section that guides yarn up onto working area.
C. Working area - section where stitches are worked.
D. Finger hold - indented section for gripping hook with your thumb and index or third finger.
E. Handle - balancing end that rests under remaining fingers or lays over hand.

The size of a hook is determined by the diameter of its working area. In addition to being measured in millimeters ***(abbreviated mm)***, each size is also assigned a letter. There can be some duplication of sizes with different letters or millimeters assigned according to what company made the hook. Lettered hooks range from size B (2.25 mm), the smallest, to size Q (15 mm), the largest.

The **more advanced** the letter, the **larger** the hook.

MATERIALS

A. Aluminum is a very popular material used for manufacturing crochet hooks. They have a smooth finish and rarely bend or break.

B. Plastic hooks are lightweight and can be found in all sizes, particularly the larger sizes, like N thru Q.

C. Wood hooks are more available than in the past and are made from some wonderful materials. They can develop burrs that can catch the yarn, but can be smoothed out with an emery board.

Steel crochet hooks are primarily used when working with threads and finer yarns. The diameters of steel hooks range from size 00 (3.5 mm) to 14 (.75 mm). With steel hooks, the larger the number is, the smaller the diameter of the hook is.

OTHER GOODIES

1. GAUGE RULER—One of the most important tools for a crocheter is the gauge ruler. It is placed on your piece so you can count your stitches and rows to check what gauge you are crocheting ***(see Gauge, page 40)***. It also has a row of holes that you can insert unmarked hooks through to determine their size.

2. MARKERS—Split or spring-shaped markers can be attached to an individual stitch to indicate the beginning of a round, the right side of a piece, or where to join yarn for stitch placement.

3. ROW COUNTER—A great accessory for you if you are crocheting a pattern with a lot of row repeats. It can be set on a table or in your lap. While it is not automatic, a row counter can be a big help in keeping track of the rows you have crocheted.

4. BOBBINS—Wind small amounts of yarn on these for use in color changes across small areas.

You'll need a bag to hold all these goodies and all the other necessities of a crocheter's life—like pen and paper, scissors (**5**), tape measure (**6**), yarn needles (**7**), and yarn threader.

And yarn, of course! *See Yarn, page 32.*

YARN

Yarn weight is divided into six basic categories. Corresponding icons are found on most yarn labels. Other names the weights may also be called are listed below.

- Super Fine; also Sock, Fingering, Baby

- Fine; also Sport, Baby

- Light; also DK, Light Medium

- Medium; also Medium, Afghan, Aran

- Bulky; also Chunky, Craft, Rug

- Super Bulky; also Bulky, Roving

Older patterns may refer to a two- or a four-ply yarn. "Ply" is the number of strands that are twisted together to make a yarn and isn't a real indication of the weight. In the past, four-ply was usually a worsted or Medium weight yarn, but now four-ply can range from Super Fine to Super Bulky. The **only** way to know what yarn to use for a pattern with unknown weight of yarn is to compare the gauge given on the label to the one in the pattern. Once you have determined the weight, any brand of yarn that is the same weight can be used. You may want to buy a skein to experiment with and crochet a gauge swatch to see how the yarn looks in the pattern.

DYE LOTS

Yarn is dyed in large batches called "dye lots." Each dye lot is assigned a number which is printed on the yarn label. Since the color may vary in shade from one dye lot to another, be sure to select enough yarn with one identical number to complete your project. It doesn't hurt to buy an extra skein, just to be on the safe side.

FIBERS

Yarn is spun and sold in a variety of fibers.

Wool is warm, naturally elastic, and holds the shape of any project well. Wool should be hand washed or dry cleaned. 100% wool will felt ***(see Felted Bag, page 58 and Felting Basics, page 45)***, unless it is a "superwash" wool, which is processed to prevent felting.

Acrylic is most times less expensive and can be usually machine washed and dried, but check the label first.

Cotton is cool, with very little elasticity. Cotton should be hand washed.

Silk is strong and also has little elasticity. You should dry clean silk.

Many yarns are a blend of fibers, such as a wool/acrylic blend. Check the skein wrapper for content and proper care instructions.

YARN TIPS

WINDING YARN INTO A BALL

Many yarns come in "pull-skeins," where the yarn is pulled from the center of the skein. In this form, it is easy to keep clean and less likely to tangle or unwind too quickly. Other yarns are sold in hanks that must be wound into balls before they are ready for use. Remove the label and unfold the hank to form a circle. Slip the yarn over the back of a chair and cut the knot that holds the strands together. Gently wrap the yarn around two fingers until a small ball is formed. Remove your fingers and continue to wind the yarn very loosely, rotating to keep the ball uniform. Be careful to wind the ball loosely, for if the yarn is pulled too tightly or stretched while being wound, it will lose some of its elasticity.

HELPFUL CHARTS

These are charts that can be found in most Leisure Arts crochet leaflets. The Crochet Terminology Chart lists equivalent international and American terms. You may have noticed symbols on yarn wrappers and in the materials paragraph in instructions; the second chart explains those. The last chart lists equivalent hook sizes.

CROCHET TERMINOLOGY		
UNITED STATES		**INTERNATIONAL**
slip stitch (slip st)	=	single crochet (sc)
single crochet (sc)	=	double crochet (dc)
half double crochet (hdc)	=	half treble crochet (htr)
double crochet (dc)	=	treble crochet (tr)
treble crochet (tr)	=	double treble crochet (dtr)
double treble crochet (dtr)	=	triple treble crochet (ttr)
triple treble crochet (tr tr)	=	quadruple treble crochet (qtr)
skip	=	miss

Yarn Weight Symbol & Names	SUPER FINE 1	FINE 2	LIGHT 3	MEDIUM 4	BULKY 5	SUPER BULKY 6
Type of Yarns in Category	Sock, Fingering Baby	Sport, Baby	DK, Light Worsted	Worsted, Afghan, Aran	Chunky, Craft, Rug	Bulky, Roving
Crochet Gauge Ranges in Single Crochet to 4" (10 cm)	21-32 sts	16-20 sts	12-17 sts	11-14 sts	8-11 sts	5-9 sts
Advised Hook Size Range	B-1 to E-4	E-4 to 7	7 to I-9	I-9 to K-10.5	K-10.5 to M-13	M-13 and larger

CROCHET HOOKS													
U.S.	B-1	C-2	D-3	E-4	F-5	G-6	H-8	I-9	J-10	K-10½	N	P	Q
Metric - mm	2.25	2.75	3.25	3.5	3.75	4	5	5.5	6	6.5	9	10	15

FAQ

My pattern said that 12 ounces of yarn was used to complete it. I bought 4 balls of yarn that had 3 ounces in each of them and I ran out of yarn! I didn't lose gauge, so did the pattern list the ounces incorrectly?

ANSWER

Sorry, you got caught in the ounces vs. yards dilemma. Yarns can weigh the same but have different lengths. You need to compare the yards (meters) of the two yarns. If the yarn you chose had 210 yards (192 meters) per ball and the pattern yarn had 250 yards (229 meters), then you were 160 yards (146 meters) short. So if you choose a different brand of yarn from the one in your pattern, you'll have to do a little math to ensure that you will have enough. Add all the yards (meters) of the pattern yarn together and then compare the sum to all the yards (meters) of the yarn you have. If your pattern doesn't list all the information about the yarn, but gives its brand name, you may be able to find out all the information about it on the Internet or by contacting the yarn company.

ADDITIONAL TECHNIQUES

Here is a sampling of techniques and stitch variations you may encounter as you practice and grow in the craft of crochet.

ADDING NEW YARN AND CHANGING COLORS

Whether you are adding new yarn or simply changing colors, there are several methods for making this happen. Whenever possible, attach new yarn at the **end** of a row or round by joining within the last stitch.

JOINING WITHIN A STITCH

This method of attaching yarn, whether to change color or simply add new yarn, may be used in the **middle** or at the **end** of a row or round. Work the last stitch to within one step of completion, hook the new yarn ***(Figs. 46a or b)***, and draw through all loops on the hook. Cut the old yarn and work over both ends unless indicated otherwise; then you will carry the old yarn along the edge of the piece to be used again a couple of rows or rounds later.

Fig. 46a

Fig. 46b

JOINING WITH SLIP STITCH

Begin with a slip knot on your hook. Insert hook in the stitch or space indicated, yarn over and draw through the stitch or space **and** the loop on the hook ***(Figs. 47a & b)***.

Fig. 47a

Fig. 47b

JOINING WITH SINGLE CROCHET

Begin with a slip knot on your hook. Insert hook in the stitch or space indicated, yarn over and pull up a loop, yarn over and draw through both loops on the hook ***(Figs. 48a & b)***.

Fig. 48a

Fig. 48b

BACK OR FRONT LOOP ONLY

When your instructions read "work Back Loops Only" or "Front Loops Only," work only in the loop(s) indicated by arrow ***(Fig. 49)***. Otherwise, work under both loops.

Fig. 49

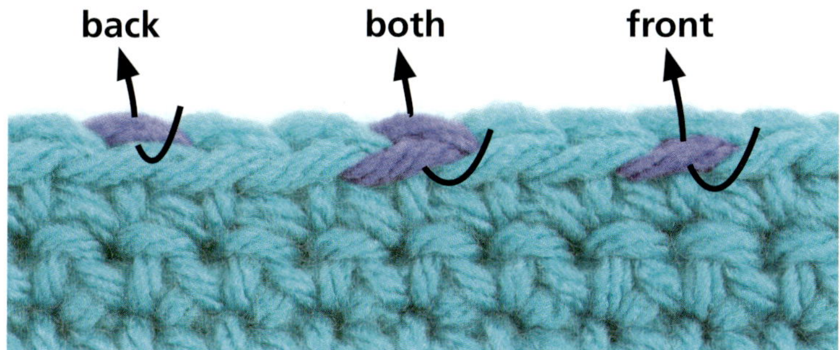

BACK OR FRONT POST STITCHES

Post stitches add texture to crochet. Work around the post of stitch indicated, inserting the hook in direction of arrow ***(Fig. 50)***.

Fig. 50 front **back**

FREE LOOPS

After working in the Back or Front Loops Only on a row or round ***(Fig. 49)***, there will be a ridge of unused loops. These are called the free loops. Later, when you are instructed to work in the free loops of the same row or round, work in these loops ***(Fig. 51)***.

Fig. 51

When your instructions read to work in the free loops of a chain, work in loop indicated by arrow ***(Fig. 52)***.

Fig. 52

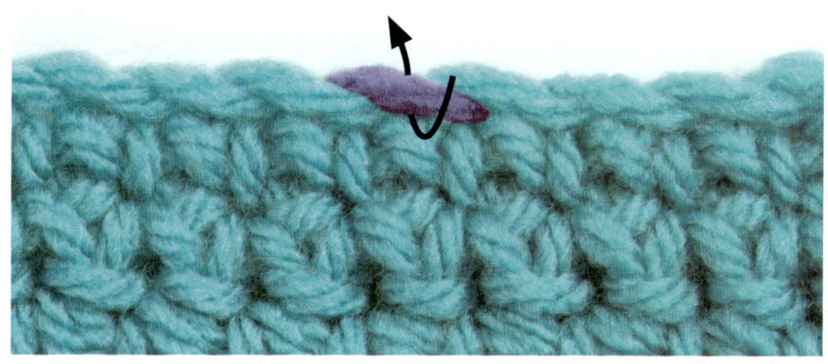

DECREASES

Decreases are used for shaping. They reduce the number of stitches and make the piece narrower.

When a decrease is used in a pattern stitch, the instructions are usually included for that specific decrease. Each basic stitch, however, has its own method of decreasing by combining two stitches into one.

SINGLE CROCHET DECREASE

(abbreviated sc decrease)

Insert hook in **next** stitch, yarn over and pull up a loop (2 loops on hook), insert hook in **next** stitch, yarn over and pull up a loop (3 loops on hook) ***(Fig. 53a)***, yarn over and draw through **all** 3 loops on the hook at once ***(Fig. 53b,* single crochet decrease made)**. The decrease counts as one single crochet.

Fig. 53a

Fig. 53b

Note: You may also complete a single crochet decrease by simply skipping a stitch. However, this is **not** recommended for the remaining basic stitches, because undesirable holes will be created.

HALF DOUBLE CROCHET DECREASE

(abbreviated hdc decrease)

Yarn over, insert hook in **next** stitch, yarn over and pull up a loop (3 loops on hook), yarn over, insert hook in **next** stitch, yarn over and pull up a loop (5 loops on hook) ***(Fig. 54a)***, yarn over and draw through **all** 5 loops on the hook at once ***(Fig. 54b,* half double crochet decrease made)**. The decrease counts as one half double crochet.

Fig. 54a

Fig. 54b

DOUBLE CROCHET DECREASE

(abbreviated dc decrease)

Yarn over, insert hook in **next** stitch, yarn over and pull up a loop, yarn over and draw through first 2 loops on hook (2 loops remaining on hook), yarn over, insert hook in **next** stitch, yarn over and pull up a loop, yarn over and draw through next 2 loops on hook (3 loops remaining on hook) ***(Fig. 55a)***, yarn over and draw through **all** 3 loops on the hook at once ***(Fig. 55b,* double crochet decrease made)**. The decrease counts as one double crochet.

Fig. 55a

Fig. 55b

TREBLE CROCHET DECREASE
(abbreviated tr decrease)

Yarn over twice, insert hook in **next** stitch, yarn over and pull up a loop, yarn over and draw through first 2 loops on hook, yarn over and draw through next 2 loops on hook (2 loops remaining on hook), yarn over twice, insert hook in **next** stitch, yarn over and pull up a loop, yarn over and draw through first 2 loops on hook, yarn over and draw through next 2 loops on hook (3 loops remaining on hook) ***(Fig. 56a)***, yarn over and draw through **all** 3 loops on the hook at once ***(Fig. 56b,* treble crochet decrease made)**. The decrease counts as one treble crochet.

Fig. 56a

Fig. 56b

INCREASES

Increases are used to add stitches to enlarge a circle, create shaping to make a piece wider, or to round corners.

An increase is the addition of a stitch so that you have two stitches worked into one stitch. To ease around a corner, there may be an increase of three stitches worked into the same stitch.

Whether you are working a single crochet, half double crochet, double crochet, or treble crochet, the increase will be made by working two or more of the same stitch into a single stitch or space. For example, **Fig. 57** shows a single crochet increase.

Fig. 57

When an increase is used in a pattern stitch, the instructions are usually included for that specific increase.

ADDING ON SINGLE CROCHET

When instructed to add on a single crochet at the end of a row, insert hook into the stitch at the base of last single crochet made ***(Fig. 58)***, yarn over and pull up a loop, yarn over and draw through **one** loop on hook, then yarn over and draw through **both** loops on hook **(single crochet added on)**. Repeat as many times as instructed.

Fig. 58

RIGHT OR WRONG SIDE

The **right** side of your work (the side that will show) is generally a matter of personal preference, but the suggested right side will usually be indicated in the pattern instructions. If right side is not denoted in instructions, then follow the guidelines listed below:

1. When working in rounds without turning, the side facing you as you work is always the "right" side.
2. When working in rows, the last row usually determines the "right" side.

Please refer to Photos A and B. Both are the same piece photographed from different sides. **Photo A** shows the "right" side facing; **Photo B** shows the "wrong" side. Notice the very smooth edge on the piece in Photo A, then compare that to the bumpy edge in Photo B. That smooth edge (the last round), clearly defined in Photo A, denotes the "right" side.

Photo A **Right side**

Photo B **Wrong side**

UNDERSTANDING INSTRUCTIONS

Crochet instructions really look like a foreign language, full of abbreviations, punctuation marks, and other terms and symbols. This method of writing saves time and space, and is actually easy to read once you understand the crochet shorthand.

ABBREVIATIONS

A list of abbreviations will be included with each leaflet or pattern, and you should review this list carefully before beginning a project. The abbreviations, symbols, and terms most frequently used by ***Leisure Arts*** are listed below.

BP	Back Post
BPdc	Back Post double crochet(s)
BPtr	Back Post treble crochet(s)
CC	Contrasting Color
ch(s)	chain(s)
cm	centimeters
dc	double crochet(s)
FP	Front Post
FPdc	Front Post double crochet(s)
FPtr	Front Post treble crochet(s)
hdc	half double crochet(s)
LSC	Long Single Crochet(s)
MC	Main Color
mm	millimeters
Rnd(s)	Round(s)
sc	single crochet(s)
sp(s)	space(s)
st(s)	stitch(es)
tr	treble crochet(s)
YO	yarn over

SYMBOLS AND TERMS

★ — used to shorten instructions. Work all instructions following a ★ (star) as many **more** times as indicated in addition to the first time.

† to † — used to shorten instructions. Work all instructions from the first † (dagger) to the second † **as many** times as specified.

multiple — the number of stitches required to complete one repeat of a pattern.

post — the vertical shaft of a stitch.

right vs. left — the side of the garment as if you were wearing it.

right side vs. wrong side — the right side of your work is the side that will show when the piece is finished.

work across or around — continue working in the established pattern.

PUNCTUATION

When reading crochet instructions, read from punctuation mark to punctuation mark. Just as in grammar, commas (,) mean pause and semicolons (;) mean stop.

colon (:) — the number(s) given after a colon at the end of a row or round denote(s) the number of stitches you should have on that row or round.

braces { } — contain information pertaining to multiple sizes.

parentheses ( ) or brackets [ ] — indicate repetition, so work the enclosed instructions **as many** times as specified by the number outside them. **Example:** "**[**sc in next sc, (3 dc in next st, ch 3) 3 times**]** twice," means that the instructions within the parentheses are to be worked 3 times and the entire sequence enclosed by the brackets is worked a total of two times. Parentheses or brackets may also indicate that several stitches are to be worked as a unit, so you should work all enclosed instructions in the stitch or space indicated. **Example:** "(sc, 2 dc, sc) in next ch-2 sp," means that **all** the stitches inside the parentheses should be worked into the next chain 2 space. Parentheses or brackets may also contain explanatory remarks.

READING PATTERNS

Let's see how crochet instructions look when written in their abbreviated form. Below are two examples of instructions. Under each example, a "translation" of how to read the example is given.

Instructions — Ch 28 **loosely**.

Translation — Make a slip knot, then make 28 chain stitches that are loose enough to work back into.

Instructions — **Row 1** (Right side)**:** Dc in fourth ch from hook **(3 skipped chs count as first dc)**, skip next ch, sc in next ch, ★ skip next ch, 3 dc in next ch, skip next ch, sc in next ch; repeat from ★ across to last 2 chs, skip next ch, 2 dc in last ch: 25 sts.

Translation — Make one double crochet in the fourth chain from the hook. (Note that the three chains you just skipped will count as the first double crochet of the row). Skip the next chain, then make one single crochet in the next chain. ★ Skip the next chain, make three double crochets all in the next chain, skip the next chain, and make one single crochet in the next chain; repeat each step after the ★ (all the instructions between the star and the semi-colon) across the chain until only two chains remain. Skip the next chain and make two double crochets all in the last chain. You now have a total of 25 stitches.

ZEROS

To shorten the length of a complex pattern, zeros are sometimes used so that all sizes can be combined. For example, "dc in next 2{0-3} stitches" means the first size would work a double crochet in next 2 stitches, the second size would do nothing, and last size would work a double crochet in the next 3 stitches.

Turn the page for more about instructions.

GAUGE

Gauge is the number of stitches and rows or rounds per inch (centimeter) and is used to determine the finished size. Most crochet patterns will specify the gauge that you must match to ensure proper size and to be sure you have enough yarn to complete the project.

Because everyone crochets differently—loosely, tightly, or somewhere in between—the finished size can vary even when crocheters use the very same pattern, yarn, and hook.

Before beginning any crocheted item, it is absolutely necessary for you to crochet a gauge swatch in the pattern stitch with the weight of yarn and hook size suggested. Your swatch must be large enough to measure your gauge, usually 4" (10 cm) square.

EXAMPLE

The pattern calls for a medium weight yarn and size H hook (5 mm) to achieve a gauge of 16 single crochets and 18 rows = 4" (10 cm).

Gauge Swatch: 4" (10 cm) square
Chain 17 **loosely**.
Row 1: Single crochet in second chain from hook and in each chain across: 16 single crochets.
Rows 2-18: Chain 1, turn; single crochet in each single crochet across.
Finish off.

Lay your swatch on a hard, smooth, flat surface. Then measure it to see if it measures 4" (10 cm). If it is **smaller** than 4" (10 cm), you are crocheting too tightly - try again with a **larger** size hook.If it is **larger** than 4" (10 cm), you are crocheting too loosely - try again with a **smaller** size hook.

Keep trying until your swatch measures 4" (10 cm) square, then use that hook to make your project.

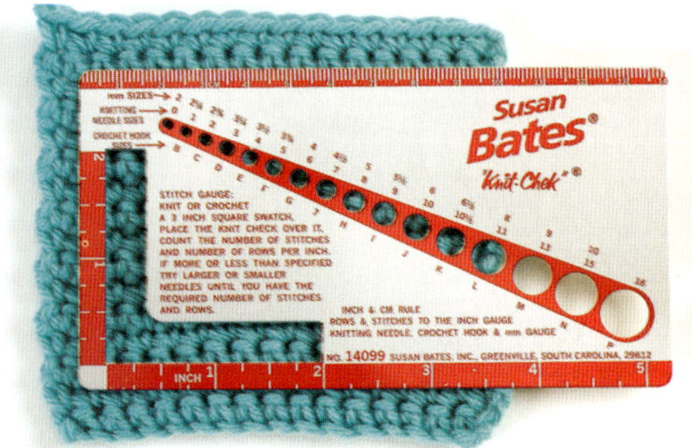

FAQ

I want to start my project now! Why do I need to waste time on a silly gauge swatch?

ANSWER

All crocheters are excited by their new projects and there are some projects where gauge doesn't matter a lot—like dishcloths or a scarf. But, if your project is supposed to fit somebody or if you want to be sure to have enough yarn, don't skip the gauge swatch. For instance, if you are crocheting a sweater with a finished measurement of 34" (86.5 cm), and your gauge is just a *little* off, say 5½ stitches per inch instead of 5, you may think that's not too bad. However, the finished sweater will measure only 31" (78.5 cm), a difference of 3" (7.5 cm) because of that extra half of a stitch per inch. If you are making an afghan, the difference would be even more dramatic.
Making an accurate gauge swatch each time you begin something new does take time. But, you don't want to spend your time working on an item that ends up several sizes too small or too large.

MARKERS

Markers are used as important reminders in a pattern ***(see Other Goodies, page 31)***.

Continuous Rounds: Markers are used to help distinguish the beginning of each round being worked. Place a marker before the first stitch of each round, moving marker after each round is complete ***(Fig. 41, page 28)***.

Right Side: When instructed to place a marker to indicate the right side, loop a short piece of yarn or attach a marker around any stitch on the side facing you **before** the work is turned.

Stitch Placement: When instructed to place a marker around a particular stitch for stitch placement (on a later row or round), be careful to mark the correct stitch. If you work in a stitch other than the one that should have been marked, the instructions may not work on the following rows or rounds.

SIZING

DECIDING WHICH SIZE TO CROCHET

First consider whether you want a loose-fitting or a snug-fitting garment when deciding on a size. Measure around the fullest part of the bust/chest and compare this measurement to the sizes given. Be sure to take an accurate measurement. Choose the size based on the actual measurement or on the finished measurement.

Most garment patterns are written for at least three different sizes. Instructions usually include actual chest/bust measurement or generic size (small, medium, large) and the finished measurement of the garment, which most times allows several inches for ease.

You may want to measure a favorite sweater with similar styling, and crochet the size that has the nearest finished measurement.

INFANTS AND CHILDREN

The only accurate way to determine which size to crochet for a child is to measure the child. Measure the child's chest approximately 2" (5 cm) below the underarm and choose the size that has the nearest actual measurement. It is also important to measure the arm length and the body length to make any necessary adjustments to the instructions.

MEASURING YOUR CROCHET

Many instructions include schematics of the garment (see below). The finished measurements of each piece are indicated for your reference so that you may accurately measure your work.

Always measure your crochet on a hard, smooth, flat surface such as a table or uncarpeted floor. Measure each piece along the lines indicated on the schematics, being careful not to stretch or bunch the piece.

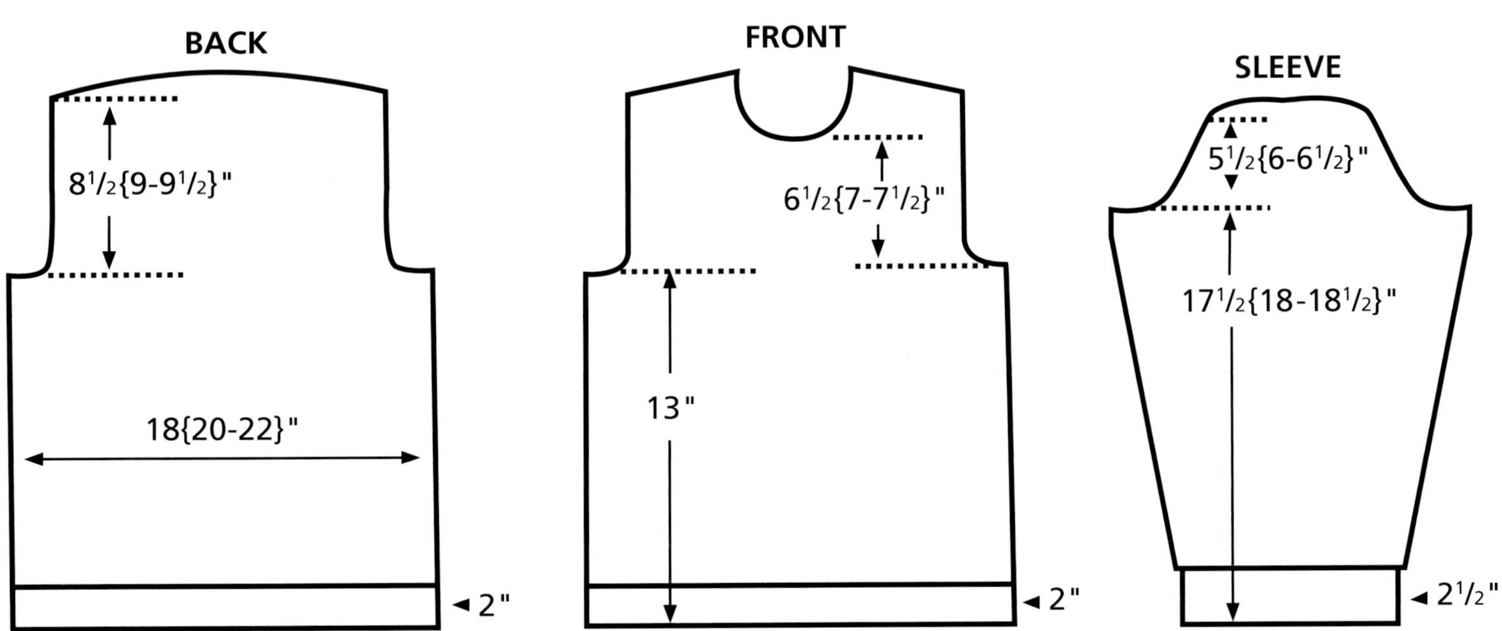

GETTING IT TOGETHER

The assembly and finishing of a design should be done with care. A crocheted item can be ruined by sloppy or incorrect finishing. The following techniques will add value and beauty to your finished work.

WEAVING IN YARN ENDS

You have finished your project, so now what to do with all the ends? You have beginning and finishing ends, and if you used more than one ball of yarn, you have those ends, too. Make a habit of taking care of loose ends as you work. Weaving in the ends gives a great result. Thread a yarn needle with the yarn end. With **wrong** side facing, weave the needle through several stitches, then reverse the direction and weave it back through several more stitches. When the end is secure, clip the yarn off close to your work. **Never** tie a knot in your yarn. A knot may poke through to the right side or become untied and you wouldn't want that!

You may also hide your ends as you work by crocheting over them for several inches to secure; clip the remaining lengths off close to your work.

Always check your work to be sure the yarn ends do not show on the right side.

SEAMS

A tapestry or yarn needle is best to use for sewing seams because the blunt point will not split the yarn. Generally, use the same yarn the item was made with to sew the seams. However, if the yarn is textured or bulky, it may be easier to sew the seam with a small, smooth yarn of the same color, such as tapestry yarn or an acrylic needlepoint yarn. If a different yarn is used for the seams, be sure the care instructions for both yarns are the same. If the yarn used to crochet the item is machine washable, the seam yarn must also be machine washable.

Any of the following techniques may be used for joining seams; however, it is usually best to weave the side and underarm seams of a garment because weaving is practically invisible and does not add bulk.

WEAVING

With **right** side of both pieces facing you and edges even, sew through both pieces once to secure the beginning of the seam, leaving an ample yarn end to weave in later. Insert the needle from **right** to **left** through one strand on each piece ***(Fig. 59)***. Bring the needle around and insert it from **right** to **left** through the next strand on both pieces. Continue in this manner, drawing seam together as you work.

Fig. 59

BACKSTITCH

Backstitch provides a firm seam. With **right** sides together and edges even, weave yarn end in securely. Insert the needle from **front** to **back** at the edge of the seam, then bring it up from **back** to **front** a half stitch forward (at 1). ★ Insert the needle back where the first stitch began (at 2) and bring it up a whole stitch forward (at 3) ***(Fig. 60a)***. Insert the needle a half stitch back from the yarn (at 1) and up again a whole stitch forward (at 4) ***(Fig. 60b)***. Repeat from ★ across the seam.

Fig. 60a

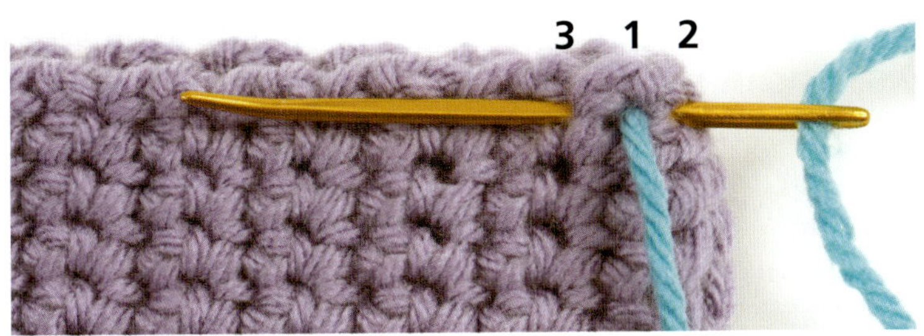

Fig. 60b

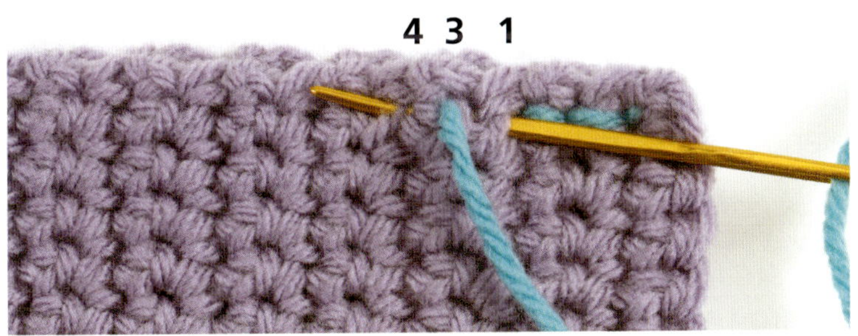

WHIPSTITCHING

Whipstitching is a very versatile finishing technique. You can whipstitch from either the right or the wrong side, using the inside loops only or both loops, and from front to back or back to front. Pattern instructions should specify the type of whipstitching to be used on a particular design. The following are just a few of the possibilities.

WHIPSTITCH ACROSS END OF ROWS

With **right** sides together, sew through both pieces once to secure the beginning of the seam, leaving an ample yarn end to weave in later. Insert the needle from **back** to **front** through one strand on each piece ***(Fig. 61)***. Bring the needle around and insert it from **back** to **front** through the next strand on both pieces.

Repeat along the edge, being careful to match stitches and rows.

Fig. 61

WHIPSTITCH THROUGH BOTH LOOPS

Place two Motifs, Squares, or Strips with **wrong** sides together. Beginning in first corner, sew through both pieces once to secure the beginning of the seam, leaving an ample yarn end to weave in later. Working through **both** loops of each stitch of **both** pieces, insert the needle from **back** to **front** through first stitch and pull yarn through ***(Fig. 62)***, ★ insert the needle from **back** to **front** through next stitch and pull yarn through; repeat from ★ across to next corner.

Fig. 62

Whipstitch continued on page 44.

WHIPSTITCH THROUGH INSIDE LOOPS

Place two Motifs, Squares, or Strips with **wrong** sides together. Beginning in center stitch on first corner, sew through both pieces once to secure the beginning of the seam, leaving an ample yarn end to weave in later. Working through **inside** loop of each stitch of **both** pieces, insert the needle from **front** to **back** through first stitch and pull yarn through ***(Fig. 63)***, ★ insert the needle from **front** to **back** through next stitch and pull yarn through; repeat from ★ across to center stitch of next corner.

Fig. 63

EDGINGS

SINGLE CROCHET EVENLY ACROSS OR AROUND

When you are instructed to single crochet evenly across or around and not given a specific number to work, you should space the single crochets out to keep the piece lying flat. Work a few single crochets at a time, checking periodically to be sure your edge is not distorted. If the edge is puckering, you need to add a few more single crochets; if the edge is ruffling, you need to remove some single crochets. Keep trying until the edge lies smooth and flat.

BLOCKING

Blocking helps smooth your work to give it a professional appearance.

Before blocking, check the yarn label for any special instructions because many acrylics and some blends may be damaged during blocking.

On acrylics that can be blocked, you simply pin your item to the correct size (with rust-proof pins), and cover the item with dampened bath towels. When the towels are dry, the item is blocked.

If the item is hand washable, carefully launder it using a mild soap or detergent. Rinse it without wringing or twisting. Remove any excess moisture by rolling it in a succession of dry towels. If you prefer, you may put it in the final spin cycle of your washer without water. Lay the item on a large towel on a flat surface out of direct sunlight. Gently smooth and pat it to the desired size and shape, comparing the measurements to the pattern instructions as necessary. When the item is completely dry, it is blocked.

Steaming is an excellent method of blocking crochet items, especially those made with wool or wool blends. Turn the item **wrong** side out and pin it to the correct size on a board covered with towels. Hold a steam iron or steamer just above the item and steam it thoroughly. Never let the weight of the iron touch your item because it will flatten the stitches. Leave the garment pinned until it is completely dry.

FELTING BASICS

Felting is simple, just 4 easy steps. All you are really doing is shrinking and changing the texture of your crocheted project!

1. START WITH WONDERFUL WOOL YARN

Read the label. AVOID "superwash" wool or wool yarns labeled as machine washable as they are made, specifically, to NOT shrink. Combining novelty yarns, like ribbon or eyelash yarns, with wool yarns can give great results. Choose a novelty yarn that can be washed in hot water. For your main (felting) yarn, chose one that is at least 50% wool. Just crochet the novelty yarn as a second strand along with the wool yarn. The wool will shrink and pull the novelty yarn with it. ***FYI:*** White and light color yarns may not felt as well as heathers or darker colors.

2. CROCHET YOUR PROJECT

ALWAYS make a test swatch. Swatch with all your yarns and colors to:

- Check crochet gauge.
- Make sure all the yarns in the project felt the way you want them to.
- Make sure the colors do not run.

3. MACHINE FELT

Set your top-loading washing machine for a HOT wash and COLD rinse cycle. Add about a tablespoon of detergent to the wash. Place the crocheted project in a tight-mesh lingerie or sweater bag and toss into the machine. Throw in an **old** pair of jeans to speed up the felting process (the more agitation, the better). Check every 2-3 minutes during the wash cycle to keep an eye on size and shrinkage of the project. A properly felted project has shrunk to the desired size and the stitches are hard to see. When checking, you may want to wear rubber gloves to protect your hands from the hot water. Once it's felted, remove it from the machine and allow the wash water to spin out. Put the project back in for the cold rinse.

4. BLOCK (Shape and dry)

Roll the felted item in a towel and gently squeeze out the excess water. Don't wring the towel as that may set in permanent creases. Form it into the size and shape by pinning to a blocking board. Let your project air dry even though it may take several days.

EMBELLISHMENTS

Sometimes, a crochet project just needs a little extra touch to be complete. Here are quick lessons on how to make fringe, pom-poms, and tassels.

FRINGE

Cut a piece of cardboard 3" (7.5 cm) wide and 1/2" (12 mm) longer than you want your finished fringe to be. Wind the yarn **loosely** and **evenly** around the cardboard lengthwise until the card is filled, then cut across one end; repeat as needed.

Hold together half as many strands of yarn as desired for the finished fringe; fold in half.

With **wrong** side facing and using a crochet hook, draw the folded end up through a stitch or space and pull the loose ends through the folded end ***(Fig. 64a)***; draw the knot up **tightly** ***(Fig. 64b)***. Repeat, spacing as desired.

Lay flat on a hard surface and trim the ends.

Fig. 64a

Fig. 64b

POM-POM

Cut a piece of cardboard 3" (7.5 cm) wide and 1 1/4" (3 cm) long. Wind the yarn around the cardboard lengthwise until it is approximately 1/2" (12 mm) thick in the middle ***(Fig. 65a)***.

Fig. 65a

Carefully slip the yarn off the cardboard and tightly tie an 18" (45.5 cm) length of yarn around the middle ***(Fig. 65b)***. Leave yarn ends long enough to attach the pom-pom. Cut the loops on both ends and trim the pom-pom into a smooth ball ***(Fig. 65c)***.

Fig. 65b

Fig. 65c

TASSEL

Cut a piece of cardboard 3" (3.75 cm) wide and as long as you want your finished tassel to be. Wind a double strand of yarn around the cardboard approximately 20 times. Cut an 18" (45.5 cm) length of yarn and insert it under all of the strands at the top of the cardboard; pull up tightly and tie securely. Leave the yarn ends long enough to attach the tassel. Cut the yarn at the opposite end of the cardboard ***(Fig. 66a)*** and then remove it.

Fig. 66a

Wrap another length of yarn tightly around the tassel twice, 1/2" (12 mm) below the top ***(Fig. 66b)***; tie securely. Trim the ends.

Fig. 66b

PROJECTS

DISHCLOTH

Finished Size: $10^1/_2$" x 10" (26.5 cm x 25.5 cm)

MATERIALS

MEDIUM 4

100% Cotton Medium Weight Yarn
[$2^1/_2$ ounces, 120 yards
(70 grams, 109 meters) per ball**]**:
Solid *(shown on page 1)* - 1 ball
Striped
White - 1 ball
Yellow - 1 ball
Crochet hook, size H (5 mm) **or** size needed for gauge

GAUGE: In pattern, 12 hdc and 7 rows = 3" (7.5 cm)

Gauge Swatch: 10"w x 3"h (25.5 cm x 7.5 cm)
Work same as Dishcloth for 7 rows.

STRIPED ONLY
Color Sequence: 2 Rows **each**: Yellow ***(Fig. 46a, page 34)***, (White, Yellow) 5 times carrying color not being used loosely along edge, changing to White at end of Row 22 and cutting Yellow.

Ch 41 **loosely**.

Row 1 (Right side)**:** Hdc in third ch from hook **(2 skipped chs count as first hdc)** and in each ch across: 40 hdc.
Rows 2-22: Ch 2 **(counts as first hdc)**, turn; ★ hdc in Back Loop Only of next hdc ***(Fig. 49, page 35)***, hdc in Front Loop Only of next hdc; repeat from ★ across to last hdc, hdc in last hdc.

Solid Only - Do **not** finish off.

EDGING

Rnd 1: Ch 1, turn; 3 sc in first hdc, sc in each hdc across to last hdc, 3 sc in last hdc; sc evenly across end of rows ***(see Edgings, page 44)***; working in free loops of beginning ch ***(Fig. 52, page 35)***, 3 sc in first ch, sc in next 38 chs, 3 sc in next ch; sc evenly across end of rows; join with slip st to first sc, finish off.

SCARF

Finished Size: $6^{3}/_{4}$"w x 41"h (17 cm x 104 cm)

MATERIALS

Medium Weight Yarn (MEDIUM 4)
[$3^{1}/_{2}$ ounces, 166 yards,
(100 grams, 152 meters) per ball]:
Burgundy - 1 ball
Lt Pink - 1 ball
Rose - 1 ball
Crochet hook, size H (5 mm) **or** size needed for gauge

GAUGE: In pattern, 13 sts and 18 rows = 4" (10 cm)

Gauge Swatch: $6^{3}/_{4}$"w x 4"h (17.25 cm x 10 cm)
Work same as Scarf for 18 rows.

STITCH GUIDE

LONG SINGLE CROCHET ***(abbreviated LSC)***
Working **around** next sc, insert hook in st one row **below**, YO and pull up a loop even with loop on hook, YO and draw through both loops on hook ***(Fig. 67)***. Skip sc under LSC.

Fig. 67

With Burgundy, ch 23 **loosely**.

Row 1 (Right side)**:** Sc in back ridge of second ch from hook ***(Fig. 11a, page 9)*** and each ch across changing to Lt Pink in last sc ***(Fig. 46a, page 34)***: 22 sc.

Note: Loop a short piece of yarn around any stitch to mark Row 1 as **right** side.

Row 2: Ch 1, turn; sc in first 2 sc, **[**work LSC ***(Fig. 67)***, sc in next sc**]** across changing to Rose in last sc.
Row 3: Ch 1, turn; sc in first 2 sc, (work LSC, sc in next st) across changing to Burgundy in last sc.
Row 4: Ch 1, turn; sc in first 2 sc, (work LSC, sc in next st) across changing to Lt Pink in last sc.

Repeat Rows 2-4 until Scarf measures $40^{1}/_{2}$" (103 cm) from beginning ch, ending by working Row 3.

Last Row: Ch 1, turn; sc in first 2 sc, (work LSC, sc in next sc) across; finish off.

Holding four strands of Burgundy, each 16" (40.5 cm) long, add fringe evenly across short edges of Scarf ***(Figs. 64a & b, page 46)***.

REVERSIBLE AFGHAN

Finished Size: 48"w x 67"h (122 cm x 170 cm)

MATERIALS

Solid Afghan Only

Medium Weight Yarn
[3½ ounces, 210 yards
(100 grams, 193 meters) per ball**]**:
18 balls
Crochet hook, size H (5 mm) **or** size needed for gauge

Striped Afghan Only

Medium Weight Yarn
[3½ ounces, 210 yards
(100 grams, 193 meters) per ball**]**:
6 balls **each**: Ecru, Blue, Lt Blue, Dk Blue
Crochet hook, size P (10 mm) **or** size needed for gauge

Note: The Striped Afghan is worked holding **two** strands of yarn together, and the Solid Afghan is worked holding only **one** strand. Instructions are written for the Striped Afghan with instructions for the Solid Afghan in braces { }. If only one number is given, it applies to both Afghans. Each row is worked across length of Afghan on either pattern.

GAUGE: For Striped Afghan Only,
9 sts and 6 rows = 4" (10 cm)
For Solid Afghan Only,
15 sts and 10 rows = 4" (10 cm)

Gauge Swatch: 4" (10 cm) square
Ch 10{16}.
Work same as Afghan for 6{10} rows.
Finish off.

Striped ONLY

Color Sequence: One row Ecru ***(Fig. 46a, page 34)***, 2 rows **each**: Lt Blue, Blue, Dk Blue, ★ Ecru, Lt Blue, Blue, Dk Blue; repeat from ★ 7 times **more**, then work one row Ecru.

Ch 150{252} **loosely**.

Row 1 (Right side)**:** Sc in back ridge of second ch from hook ***(Fig. 11a, page 9)*** and each ch across: 149{251} sc.

Note: Loop a short piece of yarn around any stitch to mark Row 1 as **right** side.

Row 2: Ch 1, turn; sc in first sc, (dc in next sc, sc in next sc) across: 149{251} sts.
Row 3: Ch 1, turn; working in Back Loops Only ***(Fig. 49, page 35)***, sc in first sc, (dc in next dc, sc in next sc) across.
Row 4: Ch 1, turn; working in both loops, sc in first sc, (dc in next dc, sc in next sc) across.
Rows 5-71{119}: Repeat Rows 3 and 4, 33{57} times; then repeat Row 3 once **more**.
Row 72{120}: Ch 1, turn; sc in both loops of each st across; finish off.

Holding 6{4} strands of corresponding color together, each 16" (40.5 cm) long, add fringe evenly across short edges of Afghan ***(Figs. 64a & b, page 46)***.

Design by Jennine Korejko.

VEST

Size	Finished Chest Measurement
X-Small	$34^1/_2$" (87.5 cm)
Small	38" (96.5 cm)
Medium	$41^3/_4$" (106 cm)
Large	$46^3/_4$" (119 cm)

Size Note: Instructions are written for size X-Small with sizes Small, Medium, and Large in braces { }. Instructions will be easier to read if you circle all the numbers pertaining to your size. If only one number is given, it applies to all sizes.

MATERIALS

MEDIUM 4

Medium Weight Yarn
[$3^1/_2$ ounces, 223 yards
(100 grams, 204 meters) per ball]:

Solid Vest
- Orange - 2{3-4-4} balls
- Brown (for Edging only) - 1 ball

Striped Vest
- Orange - 1{2-2-2} ball(s)
- Green - 1{2-2-2} ball(s)
- Dk Green (for Edging only) - 1 ball

Crochet hook, size I (5.5 mm) **or** size needed for gauge
Yarn needle

GAUGE: 13 sc and 16 rows = 4" (10 cm)

Gauge Swatch: 4" (10 cm) square.
With Orange, ch 14.
Row 1: Sc in second ch from hook and in each ch across: 13 sc.
Rows 2-16: Ch 1, turn; sc in each sc across.
Finish off.

STITCH GUIDE

BEGINNING DECREASE
Ch 1, turn; pull up a loop in each of first 2 sc, YO and draw through all 3 loops on hook **(counts as first sc)**.

DECREASE
Pull up a loop in each of next 2 sc, YO and draw through all 3 loops on hook ***(Figs. 53a & b, page 36)*** **(counts as one sc)**.

LONG SINGLE CROCHET ***(abbreviated LSC)***
Working **around** previous rows, insert hook in sc 2 rows **below** next sc ***(Fig. 68a)*** **or** in second sc **below** sc at end of next row ***(Fig. 68b)***, YO and pull up a loop even with loop on hook, YO and draw through both loops on hook.

REVERSE SINGLE CROCHET ***(abbreviated reverse sc)***
Working from **left** to **right**, ★ insert hook in sc to right of hook, YO and draw through, under and to left of loop on hook (2 loops on hook), YO and draw through both loops on hook ***(Figs. 71a-d, page 63)***; repeat from ★ across.

Fig. 68a

Fig. 68b

STRIPED VEST - COLOR SEQUENCE

Size X-Small Only - 6 rows **each**: (Orange, Green) 6 times.

Size Small Only - 6 rows **each**: (Orange, Green) 6 times; then 2 rows Orange.

Size Medium Only - 6 rows **each**: (Orange, Green) 6 times; then 4 rows Orange.

Size Large Only - 6 rows **each**: Orange, (Green, Orange) 6 times; then 2 rows Green.

SOLID VEST - Use Orange until Edging.

BODY

Vest is worked in one piece to the armhole shaping.

With Orange, ch 113{125-137-153}.

Row 1 (Right side)**:** Sc in second ch from hook and in each ch across: 112{124-136-152} sc.

Note: Loop a short piece of yarn around any stitch to mark Row 1 as **right** side.

Rows 2-38: Ch 1, turn; sc in each sc across.

Do **not** finish off.

Vest continued on page 54.

RIGHT FRONT

Row 39: Ch 1, turn; sc in first 26{29-32-36} sc, leave remaining 86{95-104-116} sc unworked.
Rows 40 and 41: Ch 1, turn; sc in each sc across to last 2 sc, decrease: 24{27-30-34} sc.
Row 42: Ch 1, turn; sc in each sc across.
Rows 43-45: Ch 1, turn; sc in each sc across to last 2 sc, decrease: 21{24-27-31} sc.
Rows 46-49: Repeat Rows 42-45: 18{21-24-28} sc.
Rows 50 and 51: Ch 1, turn; sc in each sc across.
Row 52: Ch 1, turn; sc in each sc across to last 2 sc, decrease: 17{20-23-27} sc.
Row 53: Ch 1, turn; sc in each sc across.
Rows 54 thru 58{64-70-78}: Repeat Rows 52 and 53, 2{5-8-12} times; then repeat Row 52 once **more**: 14 sc.
Rows 59{65-71-79} thru 72{74-76-80}: Ch 1, turn; sc in each sc across.
Finish off leaving a long end for sewing.

BACK

Row 39: With **right** side facing and working in unworked sc on Row 38, skip first 4 sc from Right Front and join yarn with sc in next sc ***(Figs. 48a & b, page 35)***; sc in next 51{57-63-71} sc, leave remaining 30{33-36-40} sc unworked: 52{58-64-72} sc.
Row 40: Ch 1, turn; sc in each sc across.
Row 41: Work beginning decrease, sc in next sc and in each sc across to last 2 sc, decrease: 50{56-62-70} sc.
Rows 42-49: Repeat Rows 40 and 41, 4 times: 42{48-54-62} sc.
Rows 50 thru 72{74-76-80}: Ch 1, turn; sc in each sc across.
Finish off.

LEFT FRONT

Row 39: With **right** side facing and working in unworked sc on Row 38, skip first 4 sc from Back and join yarn with sc in next sc; sc in next sc and in each sc across: 26{29-32-36} sc.
Rows 40 and 41: Work beginning decrease, sc in next sc and in each sc across: 24{27-30-34} sc.
Row 42: Ch 1, turn; sc in each sc across.
Rows 43-45: Work beginning decrease, sc in next sc and in each sc across: 21{24-27-31} sc.
Rows 46-49: Repeat Rows 42-45: 18{21-24-28} sc.
Rows 50 and 51: Ch 1, turn; sc in each sc across.
Row 52: Work beginning decrease, sc in next sc and in each sc across: 17{20-23-27} sc.
Row 53: Ch 1, turn; sc in each sc across.
Rows 54 thru 58{64-70-78}: Repeat Rows 52 and 53, 2{5-8-12} times; then repeat Row 52 once **more**: 14 sc.
Rows 59{65-71-79} thru 72{74-76-80}: Ch 1, turn; sc in each sc across.
Finish off leaving a long end for sewing.

Using long ends, whipstitch shoulder seams ***(Fig. 62, page 43)***.

EDGINGS

LONG SC *(shown on Solid Vest)*

BODY

With **right** side facing, join Brown with slip st in any sc at center Back neck; ch 1, (work LSC, ch 1) evenly around ***(see Edgings, page 44)***, working (LSC, ch 1) 3 times in each corner; join with slip st to first LSC, finish off.

ARMHOLE

With **right** side facing, join Brown with slip st in any sc on either armhole; ch 1, work (LSC, ch 1) evenly around; join with slip st to first LSC, finish off.

Repeat for second armhole.

REVERSE SC *(shown on Striped Vest)*

BODY

Rnd 1: With **right** side facing, join Dk Green with sc in sc at center Back neck; sc evenly around entire Vest ***(see Edgings, page 44)***, working 3 sc in each corner; join with slip st to first sc.
Rnd 2: Ch 1, working from **left** to **right**, work reverse sc in each sc around ***(Figs. 71a-d, page 63)***; join with slip st to first st, finish off.

ARMHOLE

Rnd 1: With **right** side facing, join Dk Green with sc in any sc on either armhole; sc evenly around; join with slip st to first sc.
Rnd 2: Ch 1, working from **left** to **right**, work reverse sc in each sc around; join with slip st to first st, finish off.

Repeat for second armhole.

KOALA BEAR

Shown on page 57.
Finished Size: 8½" (21.5 cm) high

MATERIALS
Medium Weight Yarn (MEDIUM 4)
[3 ounces, 153 yards,
(85 grams, 140 meters) per skein**]**:
Tan - 1 skein
White - 25 yards (23 meters)
Black - 10 yards (9 meters)
Crochet hook, size H (5 mm) **or** size needed for gauge
Polyester fiberfill
Yarn needle

GAUGE: Rnds 1-3 of Head = 1½" (3.75 cm)
7 sc and 7 rows = 2" (5 cm)

STITCH GUIDE

DECREASE
Pull up a loop in each of next 2 sc, YO and draw through all 3 loops on hook ***(Figs. 53a & b, page 36)*** **(counts as one sc)**.
LOOP STITCH *(abbreviated Loop St)*
Insert hook in next st, wrap yarn around index finger of left hand 2 times **more**, insert hook through all loops on finger following direction indicated by arrow ***(Fig. 69a)***, carefully hook all loops ***(Fig. 69b)***, draw through st, remove finger from loops, YO and draw through all 4 loops on hook pulling each loop to measure approximately 1"(2.5 cm) **(Loop St made, *Fig. 69c*)**.

Fig. 69a

Fig. 69b

Fig. 69c

HEAD

With Tan, ch 3 **loosely**; being careful not to twist ch, join with slip st to form a ring.

Rnd 1 (Right side)**:** 2 Sc in each ch around; do **not** join, place marker ***(see Continuous Rounds, page 28, and Markers, page 40)***: 6 sc.
Rnd 2: 2 Sc in each sc around: 12 sc.
Rnd 3: (Sc in next sc, 2 sc in next sc) around: 18 sc.
Rnd 4: (Sc in next 2 sc, 2 sc in next sc) around: 24 sc.
Rnd 5: (Sc in next 3 sc, 2 sc in next sc) around: 30 sc.
Rnd 6: (Sc in next 4 sc, 2 sc in next sc) around: 36 sc.
Rnds 7-16: Sc in each sc around.
Rnd 17: Decrease around; do **not** finish off: 18 sc.

Stuff Head firmly.

Koala Bear continued on page 56.

BODY

Rnd 1: Sc in each sc around: 18 sc.
Rnd 2: 2 Sc in each sc around: 36 sc.
Rnd 3: (Sc in next 5 sc, 2 sc in next sc) around: 42 sc.
Rnds 4-19: Sc in each sc around.
Rnd 20: (Sc in next 5 sc, decrease) around: 36 sc.
Rnd 21: Decrease around: 18 sc.
Rnd 22: Sc in each sc around.
Rnd 23: (Sc in next sc, decrease) around: 12 sc.
Rnd 24: Sc in each sc around.

Stuff Body firmly.

Rnd 25: Decrease around; slip st in next sc, finish off leaving a long end for sewing: 6 sc.

Thread yarn needle with end and weave through remaining stitches; gather **tightly** and secure.

EAR (Make 2)

INNER EAR

With White, ch 11 **loosely**.

Row 1 (Right side)**:** Sc in second ch from hook and in each ch across: 10 sc.
Row 2: Ch 1, turn; work 2 Loop Sts in first sc ***(Figs. 69a-c, page 55)***, work Loop St in each sc across to last sc, work 2 Loop Sts in last sc: 12 Loop Sts.
Row 3: Ch 1, turn; sc in each st across.
Row 4: Ch 1, turn; work Loop St in first sc, skip next sc, work Loop St in next 8 sc, skip next sc, work Loop St in last sc; finish off: 10 Loop Sts.

OUTER EAR

With Tan, ch 11 **loosely**.

Row 1 (Right side)**:** Sc in second ch from hook and in each ch across: 10 sc.

Note: Loop a short piece of yarn around any stitch to mark Row 1 as **right** side.

Row 2: Ch 1, turn; 2 sc in first sc, sc in each sc across to last sc, 2 sc in last sc: 12 sc.
Row 3: Ch 1, turn; sc in each sc across.
Row 4: Ch 1, turn; decrease, sc in each sc across to last 2 sc, decrease; do **not** finish off: 10 sc.
Edging (Joining rnd)**:** With **wrong** sides together, Inner Ear facing, working through both pieces, and matching sts, 2 sc in end of each row across; 2 sc in each free loop of beginning ch ***(Fig. 52, page 35)***; 2 sc in end of each row across; sc in each st across Row 4; join with slip st to first sc, finish off leaving a long end for sewing.

Using photo as a guide for placement, sew Ears to Head.

LEG (Make 2)

With Tan, ch 3 **loosely**; being careful not to twist ch, join with slip st to form a ring.

Rnd 1 (Right side)**:** 2 Sc in each ch around; do **not** join, place marker: 6 sc.
Rnd 2: 2 Sc in each sc around: 12 sc.
Rnd 3: (Sc in next sc, 2 sc in next sc) around: 18 sc.
Rnd 4: (Sc in next 2 sc, 2 sc in next sc) around: 24 sc.
Rnds 5-12: Sc in each sc around.
Rnd 13: (Sc in next 7 sc, 2 sc in next sc) around: 27 sc.
Rnd 14: (Sc in next 8 sc, 2 sc in next sc) around; slip st in next sc, finish off leaving a long end for sewing.

Using photo as a guide for placement, stuff Legs firmly and sew to Body, spacing approximately 2" (5 cm) apart in front.

ARM (Make 2)

With Tan, ch 3 **loosely**; being careful not to twist ch, join with slip st to form a ring.

Rnd 1 (Right side)**:** 2 Sc in each ch around; do **not** join, place marker: 6 sc.
Rnd 2: 2 Sc in each sc around: 12 sc.
Rnd 3: (Sc in next sc, 2 sc in next sc) around: 18 sc.
Rnds 4-12: Sc in each sc around; at end of Rnd 12, slip st in next sc, finish off leaving a long end for sewing.

Stuff Arms firmly up to 1" (2.5 cm) from top edge; lightly stuff remaining portion.

Flatten top edge of each Arm and sew opening closed. Using photo as a guide for placement, sew Arms to Body.

NOSE

Row 1: With Black, ch 2, 2 sc in second ch from hook.
Row 2 (Right side)**:** Ch 1, turn; 2 sc in each sc across: 4 sc.

Note: Mark Row 2 as **right** side and top.

Rows 3-5: Ch 1, turn; sc in each sc across.
Row 6: Ch 1, turn; decrease twice: 2 sc.

Edging: Ch 1, do **not** turn; sc in end of each row across; sc in free loop of ch at base of first sc; sc in end of each row across; sc in each sc across Row 6; join with slip st to first sc, finish off leaving a long end for sewing.

Using photo as a guide for placement, sew Nose to Head, stuffing firmly before closing.

FINISHING

Using photo as a guide for placement and 2 strands of Black, embroider eyes on Head and 3 claws over end of each Leg and Arm, using 2 straight stitches for each eye and claw.

Design by Cindy Harris.

FELTED BAG

Finished Size before felting:
16" (40.5 cm) diameter
Finished Size after felting (approximate)**:**
14" (35.5 cm) diameter

MATERIALS (see Felting Basics, page 45)

Version A

SUPER BULKY 6

50% Wool Super Bulky Weight Yarn
[1¾ ounces, 55 yards
(50 grams, 50 meters) per ball]:
Variegated (Color A) - 2 balls

MEDIUM 4

100% Wool Medium Weight Yarn
[3½ ounces, 223 yards
(100 grams, 205 meters) per ball]:
Green - 2 balls
Orange - 2 balls

Version B

MEDIUM 4

100% Wool Medium Weight Yarn
[3½ ounces, 223 yards
(100 grams, 205 meters) per ball]:
Blue (Color A) - 2 balls
Green - 2 balls
Orange - 2 balls

Crochet hook, size J (6 mm) **or** size needed for gauge
Safety pin - 2
Yarn needle

GAUGE SWATCH: Rnds 1 and 2 = 4" (10 cm)

For Version A, work with one strand of Color A or two strands of Green or two strands of Orange as specified throughout.

For Version B, work with two strands of Color A, two strands of Green, or two strands of Orange as specified throughout.

BODY (Make 2)

With Color A, ch 4; join with slip st to form a ring.

Rnd 1 (Right side)**:** Ch 3 **(counts as first dc, now and throughout)**, 11 dc in ring; join with slip st to first dc, finish off: 12 dc.

Note: Loop a short piece of yarn around any stitch to mark Rnd 1 as **right** side.

Rnd 2: With **right** side facing, join Orange with slip st in any dc; ch 3, dc in same st, 2 dc in next dc and in each dc around; join with slip st to first dc, finish off: 24 dc.
Rnd 3: With **right** side facing, join Color A with slip st in any dc; ch 3, 2 dc in next dc, (dc in next dc, 2 dc in next dc) around; join with slip st to first dc: 36 dc.
Rnd 4: Ch 3, dc in next dc, 2 dc in next dc, (dc in next 2 dc, 2 dc in next dc) around; join with slip st to first dc, finish off: 48 dc.
Rnd 5: With **right** side facing, join Green with slip st in any dc; ch 3, dc in next 2 dc, 2 dc in next dc, (dc in next 3 dc, 2 dc in next dc) around; join with slip st to first dc: 60 dc.
Rnd 6: Ch 3, dc in next 3 dc, 2 dc in next dc, (dc in next 4 dc, 2 dc in next dc) around; join with slip st to first dc, finish off: 72 dc.
Rnd 7: With **right** side facing, join Color A with slip st in any dc; ch 3, dc in next 4 dc, 2 dc in next dc, (dc in next 5 dc, 2 dc in next dc) around; join with slip st to first dc: 84 dc.
Rnd 8: Ch 3, dc in next 5 dc, 2 dc in next dc, (dc in next 6 dc, 2 dc in next dc) around; join with slip st to first dc, finish off: 96 dc.
Rnd 9: With **right** side facing, join Orange with slip st in any dc; ch 3, dc in next dc and in each dc around; join with slip st to first dc, finish off.

Felted Bag continued on page 60.

B

STRAP/GUSSET

With Orange, ch 8.

Row 1 (Right side)**:** Dc in fourth ch from hook **(3 skipped chs count as first dc)** and in each ch across: 6 dc.

Note: Mark Row 1 as **right** side.

Row 2: Ch 3, turn; dc in next dc and in each dc across.

Repeat Row 2 until Strap/Gusset measures approximately 70" (178 cm) from beginning ch, ending by working a **wrong** side row; do **not** finish off.

Edging: Ch 1, turn; sc in each dc across to last dc, 3 sc in last dc; working in end of rows, sc evenly across to beginning ch ***(see Edgings, page 44)***, working in free loops of beginning ch ***(Fig. 52, page 35)***, 3 sc in first ch, sc in next 4 chs, 3 sc in next ch, sc evenly across end of rows, 2 sc in same dc as first sc; join with slip st to first sc, finish off leaving a long end for sewing.

With **wrong** side together, being careful not to twist the piece, and matching stitches, whipstitch the short ends together ***(Fig. 62, page 43)***.

JOINING

In order to join a round piece to a straight edge, it will be necessary to ease them together by skipping sts on the straight edge. So, when joining the Body to the Gusset, work in every dc indicated on the Body, but skip sc on the Gusset when necessary.

FIRST SIDE

With **wrong** sides together and working in **both** loops on **both** pieces, join Orange with sc in any st ***(Figs. 48a & b, page 35)***; (ch 1, sc in next st) 76 times; finish off leaving 19 dc on Body unworked.

SECOND SIDE

For the opening to be even, you must begin and end the joining of the remaining Body piece in the sc opposite the beginning and ending of the First Side. To do this, with **wrong** sides together, pin one dc of the remaining Body to the corresponding sc on the Gusset Edging opposite the stitch in which the previous joining ended. Skip 19 dc from the pinned dc and pin the next dc to the corresponding sc opposite the stitch in which the previous joining began.

Join Orange with sc in first pinned dc; (ch 1, sc in next st) across to next pinned dc; finish off.

Felt Purse ***(see Felting Basics, page 45)***.

BABY AFGHAN

Finished Size: 35"w x 44"h (89 cm x 112 cm)

MATERIALS

Light Weight Yarn
[5 ounces, 455 yards
(140 grams, 416 meters) per ball]:
- Yellow - 3 balls
- White - 2 balls
- Blue - 1 ball

Crochet hook, size G (4 mm) **or** size needed for gauge
Yarn needle

GAUGE: Each Square = $4\frac{1}{4}$" (10.75 cm)

STITCH GUIDE

FRONT POST TREBLE CROCHET ***(abbreviated FPtr)***
YO twice, insert hook from **front** to **back** around post of dc indicated ***(Fig. 50, page 35)***, YO and pull up a loop, (YO and draw through 2 loops on hook) 3 times ***(Fig. 70)***.

Fig. 70

Baby Afghan instructions begin on page 62.

SQUARE (Make 80)

With Blue, ch 6; join with slip st to form a ring.

Rnd 1 (Right side)**:** Ch 1, (3 sc in ring, ch 4) 4 times; join with slip st to first sc: 12 sc and 4 ch-4 sps.

Note: Loop a short piece of yarn around any stitch to mark Rnd 1 as **right** side.

Rnd 2: Ch 1, sc in same st and in next 2 sc, (slip st, ch 9, slip st) in next ch-4 sp, ★ sc in next 3 sc, (slip st, ch 9, slip st) in next ch-4 sp; repeat from ★ 2 times **more**; join with slip st to first sc, finish off: 12 sc and 4 ch-9 sps.
Rnd 3: With **right** side facing and working **behind** ch-9, join White with slip st in any ch-4 sp on Rnd 1; ch 3 **(counts as first dc, now and throughout)**, (dc, ch 2, 2 dc) in same sp, dc in next 3 sc on Rnd 2, ★ working **behind** next ch-9, (2 dc, ch 2, 2 dc) in next ch-4 sp on Rnd 1, dc in next 3 sc on Rnd 2; repeat from ★ around; join with slip st to first dc: 28 dc and 4 ch-2 sps.
Rnd 4: Ch 3, dc in next dc, 2 dc in next ch-2 sp, dc in next ch-9 sp on **Rnd 2**, ch 9, slip st in top of dc just made, 2 dc in same sp on **Rnd 3**, dc in next 2 dc, ch 3, skip next 3 dc, ★ dc in next 2 dc, 2 dc in next ch-2 sp, dc in next ch-9 sp on **Rnd 2**, ch 9, slip st in top of dc just made, 2 dc in same sp on **Rnd 3**, dc in next 2 dc, ch 3, skip next 3 dc; repeat from ★ around; join with slip st to first dc, finish off: 36 dc and 4 ch-9 sps.

Rnd 5: With **right** side facing, join Yellow with slip st in same st as joining; ch 3, dc in next 3 dc, working **behind** next ch-9, (2 dc, ch 1, 2 dc) in same dc as ch-9, dc in next 4 dc, working in **front** of next ch-3, work FPtr around each of next 3 skipped dc on **Rnd 3** ***(Fig. 70, page 61)***, ★ dc in next 4 dc on **Rnd 4**, working **behind** next ch-9, (2 dc, ch 1, 2 dc) in same dc as ch-9, dc in next 4 dc, working in **front** of next ch-3, work FPtr around each of next 3 skipped dc on **Rnd 3**; repeat from ★ around; join with slip st to first dc: 60 sts and 4 ch-1 sps.
Rnd 6: Ch 1, sc in same st and in next 5 dc, sc in next ch-1 sp, sc in next ch-9 sp on **Rnd 4** and in same sp on **Rnd 5**, ★ sc in next 15 sts and in next ch-1 sp, sc in next ch-9 on **Rnd 4** and in same sp on **Rnd 5**; repeat from ★ 2 times **more**, sc in each st across; join with slip st to first sc, finish off: 72 sc.

FINISHING

ASSEMBLY

With Yellow and working through **inside** loops, whipstitch Squares together forming 8 vertical strips of 10 Squares each ***(Fig. 63, page 44)***, beginning in center sc of first corner and ending in center sc of next corner; then whipstitch strips together in same manner.

EDGING

Rnd 1: With **right** side facing, join Yellow with sc in any corner sc ***(Figs. 48a & b, page 35)***; 2 sc in same st, sc evenly around working 3 sc in each corner sc; join with slip st to first sc.

Rnd 2: Ch 1, working from **left** to **right**, ★ insert hook in sc to right of hook ***(Fig. 71a)***, YO and draw through, under and to left of loop on hook (2 loops on hook) ***(Fig. 71b)***, YO and draw through both loops on hook ***(Fig. 71c)*** **(reverse sc made, *Fig. 71d*)**; repeat from ★ around; join with slip st to first st, finish off.

Fig. 71a

Fig. 71b

Fig. 71c

Fig. 71d

YARN INFORMATION

Projects in this leaflet were made using various weights of yarn. Any brand of specified weight of yarn may be used. It is best to refer to the yardage/meters when determining how many balls or skeins to purchase. Remember, to arrive at the finished size, it is the GAUGE/TENSION that is important, not the brand of yarn. For your convenience, listed below are the specific yarns used to create our photography models.

DISHCLOTH

Lily® Sugar 'N Cream®
Solid
#28 Delft Blue
Striped
Yellow - #10 Yellow
White - #01 White

SCARF

Bernat® Satin
Burgundy - #04307 Sultana
Lt Pink - #04423 Flamingo
Rose - #04732 Maitai

REVERSIBLE AFGHAN

Patons® Decor
Solid
#01648 Rich Country Pink
Striped
Ecru - #01614 Winter White
Blue - #16142 Periwinkle
Lt Blue - #16143 Pale Periwinkle
Dk Blue - #16141 Rich Periwinkle

VEST

Patons® Classic Wool
Solid
#00238 Paprika
Edging - #00231 Chestnut Brown
Striped
Rust - #00238 Paprika
Green - #00240 Leaf Green
Edging - #00205 Deep Olive

KOALA BEAR

Red Heart® Classic
Tan - #334 Tan
Black - #12 Black
White - #1 White

FELTED PURSE

Version A
Lion Brand® Landscapes®
Color A (Variegated) - #281 Coral Reef
Patons® Classic Wool
Green - #00240 Leaf Green
Orange - #00238 Paprika
Version B
Patons® Classic Wool
Color A (Blue) - #77734 Too Teal
Green - #00240 Leaf Green
Orange - #00238 Paprika

BABY AFGHAN

Bernat® Softee® Baby
White - #02000 White
Blue - #30184 Denim Baby
Yellow - #02003 Lemon

INDEX

A

Abbreviations, 38
Adding new yarn
  with single crochet, 35
  with slip stitch, 34
  within stitch, 34
Adding on single crochet, 37
Afghans
  Baby, 61
  Reversible, 50
Aluminum hooks, 31

B

Back loop, 35
Back post, 35
Back ridge, 8
Backstitch, 43
Basic materials, 2, 30-31
Basic stitches
  chain, 5-7
  double crochet, 19-22
  half double crochet, 15-18
  single crochet, 10-13
  slip stitch, 14
  treble crochet, 22-26
Beginning loop, 28
Beginning ring, 28
Blocking, 44
Bobbins, 30, 31
Both loops, 35

C

Chain
  back ridge of, 9
  chaining loosely, 8
  free loops of, 35
  making a chain, 5-7
  top two loops of, 9
  turning chains, 12, 17, 21, 25, 27
  working into, 8-9
Changing colors, 34
Charts
  Crochet Terminology, 33
  Yarn Weight, 33
  Crochet Hooks, 33
Crochet hooks, 30-31

D

Decreases
  single crochet, 36
  half double crochet, 36
  double crochet, 36
  treble crochet, 37
Dishcloth, 48
Double crochet
  decrease, 36
  making, 19-22
Dye lots, 32

E

Edgings, 44

F

FAQ, 2, 4, 6, 27, 33, 40
Felted Bag, 58
Felting Basics, 45
Finish off, 15
Free loops
  of a chain, 35
  of a row/round, 35
Front loop, 35
Front post, 35
Front post treble crochet, 61
Fringe, 46

G

Gauge
  measuring, 40
  swatch, 40
Gauge ruler, 30, 31, 40

H

Half double crochet
  decrease, 36
  making, 15-18
Hooks
  anatomy of, 31
  holding, 2
  sizes, 31
  types, 30, 31

I
Increases, 37
Instructions (understanding), 38-39
Introduction, 1
J
Joining
  with single crochet, 35
  with slip stitch, 34
  within stitch, 34
K
Koala bear, 55-57
L
Left-handed (special note), 29
Long single crochet, 49, 52
Loop stitch, 55
M
Markers, 28, 30, 31, 40
  continuous rounds, 28
  right side, 40
  stitch placement, 40
Measuring
  garments, 41
  gauge, 40
N
Necessities, 30, 31
P
Plastic hooks, 31
Post stitch, 35
Punctuation, 39
R
Reading patterns, 39
Reverse single crochet, 63
Right side, 38
Rounds
  beginning loop, 28
  beginning ring, 28
  vs Rows, 27
  continuous, 28
  with turning, 29
  without turning, 29
  working in, 27-29
Row counter, 30, 31
Rows, 27
S
Scarf, 49
Seams, 42
Single crochet
  adding on, 37
  decrease, 36
  evenly, 44
  increase, 37
  joining with, 35
  long, 49, 52
  making, 10-13
Sizing, 41
Slip knot, 3
Slip stitch
  making, 14
  joining with, 34
Steel hooks, 31
Symbols, 39
T
Tape measure, 30, 31
Terms, 39
Treble crochet
  decrease, 37
  making, 22-26
Turning chains, 12, 17, 21, 25, 27
V
Vest, 52-54
W
Weaving
  seams, 42
  yarn ends, 42
Whipstitch
  across end of rows, 43
  both loops, 43
  inside loops, 44
Wood hooks, 31
Working yarn, 3
Working area of a hook, 2, 31
Wrong side, 38
Y
Yarn
  adding new, 34
  dye lots, 32
  fibers, 32
  holding, 4
  ply, 32
  types, 32
  weight, 32
Yarn ends, 42
Yarn needle, 30, 31
Yarn over, 4
Z
Zeros, 39

We have made every effort to ensure that these instructions are accurate and complete. We cannot, however, be responsible for human error, typographical mistakes, or variations in individual work.

Items made and instructions tested by JoAnn Bowling, Marianna Crowder, Raymelle Greening, and Sue Galucki.

Production Team: Instructional Editor - Sarah J. Green; Technical Editor - Cathy Hardy; Editorial Writer - Susan McManus Johnson; Graphic Artist - Amy Gerke; Senior Graphic Artist - Lora Puls; Photo Stylist - Jessica Wurst; and Photographer - Jason Masters.